Fabulous Foodie Favorites

Cook, Eat

Smile, Repeat!

by

Kitchen Kimberley

Contents:

Dedication:

To my late mother, Jo Willa Garman Graham

January 21, 1937 - December 22, 2009

This cookbook is lovingly dedicated to the memory of my sweet Mommy. She always inspired me to do more and to be better; and then when I did, she proudly bragged about it to anyone who would listen! She was my biggest fan and my best friend.

My Mommy bravely battled lung cancer on three different occasions over the last seventeen years of her life, and only lost that battle due to complications from COPD. She was an amazing woman of faith, strength, courage, love and laughter. Her generous spirit enabled her to work tirelessly to raise her four children as a military wife, and to make the necessary sacrifices to provide a loving and safe home for her family.

Over the years we shared many delightful hours in the kitchen, both cooking and laughing together. She was a wonderful Mother, and a very special friend. Her support was never-ending and her love was not only limitless but also unconditional. I am the strong woman I am today, only because of my sweet Mommy.

I miss her more than words can ever begin to express.

May you rest in peace, my sweet Mommy. I love you.

-Kimmie Jo

Acknowledgements:

First and foremost, I always give thanks to my Lord and savior, Jesus Christ. *Praise God from whom all blessings flow!*

To my sweet Terry, thank you for being my precious husband and my best friend for over 15 years now! You are such a blessing to my life, and I love every moment we spend together. Thank you for your unconditional love, laughter, support, encouragement, patience, and for always 'blessing me' by washing the never-ending dishes!   I love you more with each passing day, and look forward to spending the rest of my life with you, my precious pumpkin.   I am so proud of the Godly man you are, and I am so very blessed to be your wife!

Thank you to my siblings, Sabrina, Carol, and Allen, for being such a wonderful support system. Family means everything to me, and I am so thankful to be your little sister! Thanks for always being there for me!

To my very special Daddy, I say thank you for raising me – which encompasses more than I can begin to express! Your sweet spirit and your wit have helped mold and shape me as a person; I am thankful for your gentle "Don't fret, Pet" reminders! It has been my great honor to see you accept Christ, and to see how your spirit has been transformed since that special day. I thank God for you, and for allowing me to be your daughter!

To my Sissy in Christ, 'Foodie Judy', thank you for always showing me God's love, and for consistently reminding me of the great plans He has for both of us! You are a light, and I am so thankful that you have shined on me. Thanks for being my precious friend, and my sweet Sissy! Hard hug!

And lastly, to all of those whom I have met over the years, thank you for encouraging me as 'Kitchen Kimberley'. Thank you for making my recipes, and especially for telling me that you love them!   Thanks to my 'family' at *The News on 6* for allowing me to share recipes with all of my 'friends'! Until we eat again...happy cooking, everyone! I wish you all the very best!

-Kimberley

Fond Food and Family Memories: *My Kitchen Kimberley Story*

Many people have asked how I came to be known as "Kitchen Kimberley". Well, it is a long story, but hopefully you will find it an interesting one. Food has always been an important part of my life, from the time I was a very young girl. My love for food began at that very young age, thanks to my parents. It may have been earlier than this, but my earliest food memory was probably around the age of five…yes, five!

While growing up, we never ate out at restaurants. Instead, my Mom always cooked three complete meals every day for our family of six. Each morning she would make eggs with bacon or sausage, and toast or biscuits. We rarely had cereal, but when we did, it was served with fresh fruit on top. Personally, I was not a fan of breakfast foods while growing up, so Mom would make a grilled cheese bacon and onion sandwich for me. Me? Spoiled? No, just very loved.

Our lunches were typically sandwiches, but most of the time they included homemade fillings such as tuna fish salad, ham salad, chicken salad, or my personal favorite, pimiento cheese. These sandwiches were also layered with fresh lettuce, tomato and onion, to ensure that we ate plenty of vegetables. Another required element of our lunch was a glass of cold milk. Mom really fed us well from her tiny kitchen, and she always made sure we ate a well-balanced diet.

When it came to fresh vegetables, most of them were harvested from the huge garden we had in our backyard. My Dad gets most of the credit there! First he made his own compost for nutrients, and then he would till it into the soil until it was silky soft and the finest you could find! Oh, and then he would till it a few more times just to make sure it was ready to grow the best quality produce! He always planted lettuce, green onions, red and icicle radishes, carrots, sugar snap peas, green beans, okra, corn, potatoes, and row after row of tomatoes! I can also remember the big yellow chrysanthemums situated on each corner of the garden. They were pretty, but also practical; as companion plants, they kept hungry insects away.

My parent's hard work in the garden resulted in a bumper crop of fresh produce every year. Of course, the first of the spring produce we could pick was the lettuce, and then the green onions. Funny -- I loved green onions, even as a child. In fact, my elementary school lunch box always held a peanut butter and jelly sandwich on wheat bread, plain potato chips, an apple, and a whole, fresh green onion from our garden. I can remember eating the green onion first, and watching the other kids make funny faces at me for doing so! But these green onions were mild and sweet, not hot like the ones you get from the store; their distinctive flavor must have been a result of all that compost and tilling! Whatever it was, they were delicious and I did not have a care in the world what the other kids thought about me or my green onions, for that matter!

Speaking of sweet produce, another of my personal favorites were the tender carrots we harvested in early spring. Because they grow underground, my Dad would have to pull one up to see how they were growing. When he decided that it was not big enough for a meal, it became a snack for me!

As a child, I also had a passion for sugar snap peas. Yes, peas. But these peas were special peas. The pods were super crunchy and sweet, and tucked inside were the tiniest, most perfectly round green peas that popped as I bit into each one individually. They were fun to eat, and I still love them today, although again...there is nothing like a *homegrown* sugar snap pea. I do remember one year when we had a bumper crop – they were prolific and super sweet that year; so sweet in fact, that I couldn't keep my tiny hands off of them! Mom and Dad thought we had a bunny in the yard. Well, we sort of did...some 'bunny' was eating them, and it was me! Sorry, Dad, and thanks for growing the best crop of sugar snap peas, ever. Yum!

With all of that fresh produce growing, we harvested something every evening. Dad and I would go out to the garden after he got home from work and pick the ripe goods together. I can remember watching him dig the potatoes, and thinking what a wonderful surprise it was to see a shovel full of little potato gems come up through the big mound of dirt. It was like unearthing a hidden treasure! The best thing about those earthy potatoes was the simple way my Mom prepared them -- boiled only until tender enough to smash with a fork, and then slathered with butter, salt and pepper. Homegrown potatoes do not need a lot of fussy preparation; just enough to let the flavor come through as they literally melt in your mouth!

When I think back to the sounds of my childhood summers, I immediately remember the loud jiggle of the pressure cooker my Mom used when canning tomatoes, green beans, and pickled okra. The noise always startled me, and I remember covering my ears as I ran from the kitchen. Then, after the jars came out of the pressure cooker, I would go back into the kitchen and help Mom count the 'popping sounds' that the lids made to indicate a proper seal on each jar. We rarely had any rejects, and it was always fun to count those 'popping sounds' together with her; I think it may have helped to calm down my 'pressure cooker' nerves, too!

My Mom canned so much produce that our family was able to eat from the garden year-round. It was a treat to have home grown green beans and tomatoes when the ground was blanketed with snow! One year I can remember there being a full box of canned vegetables underneath each of our beds -- since the pantry was full, and the shelves in the garage were stacked to the ceiling, as well. That year I had the green beans under my bed; probably because I could not be trusted with the pickled okra – it would have been my midnight snack! Those were safely stored in my brother Allen's room, along with the box of tomatoes, which he would never touch, and still will not touch today! He is really missing out when it comes to tomatoes!

Needless to say, with our family's great love for fresh produce, and the abundance thereof, nothing ever went to waste, no matter how large the harvest. At times we would share with family, and other times with neighbors.

One of our neighbors, Mrs. Lane, frequently baked fresh loaves of bread in the morning. It always smelled so delicious when the delicate aromas wafted through her open window and into our backyard. When Mom was outside working in the garden, Mrs. Lane would come out and greet her with a loaf of fresh bread still warm from the oven. In exchange, Mom would share the freshest of produce from the garden with her. They passed their goods across the chain-link fence and exchanged kind words at the same time. It was a friendly gesture and a win-win for both of these hard working ladies. Over the years we enjoyed many loaves of that delicious homemade bread. Sharing brings joy to both the giver, and to the receiver!

Our dinners were always served promptly at 5:30, and each meal included a meat, a green vegetable, a starch, a salad and some type of warm bread. When it came to meal planning and cooking, my Mom was an expert. You can imagine the amount of time she spent in the kitchen making 21 meals each week for a family of 6, but she *never* complained! After so many years of countless hours in the kitchen, she was quite the experienced home cook, and she always made meal preparation look effortless.

One night while preparing dinner, Mom asked me if I wanted to help her make the salad. I was five years old! Well, of course I jumped at the chance to be a 'big girl' and help Mommy cook! She brought in a stool for me to stand on so I could comfortably reach the countertop. Then, she placed the big salad bowl in front of me along with a pile of freshly washed leaves of iceberg lettuce. She stood right beside me and chopped the celery, carrots and radishes while I tore the lettuce into tiny pieces, and together we made a beautiful dinner salad. By helping her to prepare the meal not only did I feel all grown up, but I also learned the value and importance of food preparation for the family.

When I was not in the kitchen helping Mom with the dinner salad, I enjoyed playing outside with my friends in our 'pretend kitchen' on the patio. We built a 'countertop' of sorts from stacked bricks topped with an old piece of plywood that was leftover from one of my Dad's home improvement projects. I had some old metal bowls to play with outside, which came in very handy for all the 'pretend cooking' we did! My friends and I made plenty of mud pies on that 'countertop', and we also made some really pretty (albeit inedible) salads! We would pull the leaves off of the shrubs and then toss in a few blades of grass for accent color. Then we would make a very thin mixture of mud and drizzle it over as a dressing. When I think back on how we played as 8-year olds, we were pretty creative!

Whenever my Mom finished with a tin of spices (back in the day spices came in metal tins) she would give it to me for our 'outdoor kitchen'. We would fill the empty spice can with dirt, and sprinkle it over our 'play salad' for extra seasoning. Once we were finished with our creations, we could simply toss them into the compost pile for Dad's garden. Oh, to be a kid again! We had such fun!

The older I grew, the busier I grew, it seems. I was one of those 'over-achiever' types in school who was involved in every activity possible! Although my time spent in the kitchen with Mom was pretty limited, I certainly never missed a minute at the dinner table! In fact, some of my fondest memories of growing up are of meals shared in the dining room around our family table. It was our gathering place, where we ate and visited about our day and laughed...a lot! At the same time, we were making great family memories!

On rare occasions, we ate in front of the television, but only for very special football games. I always knew that football meant we would get to sit around the console television and munch on cold fried chicken! You see, whenever there was a good weekend afternoon game, Mom made it extra special by cooking in advance so she could enjoy every minute with us. (She was a huge football fan!). My Mom battered and fried chicken the day before the game, and refrigerated it overnight to be served cold. In addition, she always made her homemade potato salad, baked beans, and deviled eggs – all dishes that tasted better the next day! Of course, there were also plenty of fresh vegetables such as celery and carrot sticks and sliced tomatoes to accompany our football feast. It was good clean, family fun, not to mention scrumptious food!

For evening snacks while watching our favorite western show, "High Chaparral", my Mom would prepare what she called a 'love plate'. It was basically a large platter full of snacks that we all shared throughout the evening – rolled up deli meats including ham and hard salami, a variety of cubed cheeses, pickled okra, black and green olives, and crackers. I enjoyed helping make our platter, because Mom always gave me a few extra black olives; in fact, I probably could have eaten the whole can all by myself! I love black olives, and still include them on the 'love plates' that I share with my hubby. Of course, he wouldn't touch them if they were the last morsel of food on Earth! It's all good -- more for me!

Although it was decades ago, I remember my 16th birthday like it was yesterday. Okay, most people do, simply because they remember going to get their drivers' license. Well, not me. What I remember most is the special birthday dinner we enjoyed together to celebrate this milestone year. On our birthdays, Mom encouraged us to select a special menu of our favorite foods for dinner. That particular year I picked a special one that everybody loved! It was one of Mom's best meals – a tender, juicy Porterhouse steak, flame-kissed by the gas broiler to a perfect medium-rare, and smothered with sautéed buttered onions. Alongside that steak sat a giant loaded baked potato, a fabulous green salad and crunchy garlic toast. And for dessert? It was my favorite cake – *Spice Cake with Cream Cheese Frosting*. Note: my birthday is in January, thus the indoor broiling instead of grilling, and my selection of a rich and heavy Spice cake!

Many of my food memories are of dinners shared with others, but always at our family table, not at restaurants. There is something so special about gathering around a family dinner table! Many of my closest friends in school loved to eat dinner at our house, because their Mom's worked and did not have time to cook homemade meals for them. My friends and I would feast on hand-breaded deep-fried chicken tenders, served with real mashed potatoes, green beans, and again, the always reliable fresh green salad, and homemade rolls. We loved to eat homemade Chocolate Chip Cookies for dessert, and they were always available, thanks to Mom. It was a joy to come in after school and smell the aroma of freshly baked cookies!

Deep-frying was a pretty common method of cooking at our house, and my Dad even got to help with that. He made the best homemade French fries ever…I can almost taste them now! Way to go, fry Daddy! Pun intended! My Mom could also fry up a mean meal of homemade corn dogs, (again, hand-breaded) and hush puppies that could knock your socks off. With a side serving of her homemade coleslaw, and sliced tomatoes from the garden, it was a meal that I will always remember fondly. To go along with those delicious corn dogs, Mom would let me make my special dipping sauce. It was nothing more than equal parts of mustard and ketchup, but when I first mixed it up at age 9, I thought I was making something pretty special!

Throughout the years some of my most prominent memories have revolved around food. From going to Mexican restaurants with a date, to developing the *Refreshing Peach Punch* recipe for my own wedding reception! From fond memories of enjoying homemade banana ice cream at our family reunions, to creating my recipe for *Pecan Pie Ice Cream*, our new family favorite. You may notice here, that all of my food memories are also related to family memories, too. Well, that is because I personally believe that food brings families together; that could not be more accurate than in my own upbringing. Sprinkled throughout this book you will read more food and family related stories on many of these special recipes.

Many people ask if I am a home economist. Well, not exactly, but I am the self-proclaimed CFO (Chief Financial Officer) of our household! My college degree is a Bachelor of Arts in Spanish from the University of Colorado at Colorado Springs. After receiving my degree, I promptly returned to Oklahoma to seek my teaching certificate. As a first year teacher of Spanish with one-hundred and thirty one 9th and 10th grade students, I quickly learned that my love for Spanish and my love for teaching were not meant to be together! While I dearly love Spanish and speak it fluently, teaching in a high school classroom is not for me. Teaching in a public school is a very tough profession – *that is an understatement* --and I genuinely admire and highly respect all of those who do it every day. Muchas gracias, profe!

In order to use my Spanish skills, I became a bilingual customer service representative for a major health insurance company. I thoroughly enjoyed that job, but in between phone calls I would daydream about what I was going to prepare for dinner that night. Food was not only a distraction for me, but also a stress-reliever! Not simply the consumption of the food, but more so the preparation of the food.

During my 'corporate years', my Aunt Jane gave me a big paper grocery sack full of recipes that had belonged to my Great Aunt Anna. Aunt Anna was one of the best cooks in our family, and over the years she had collected and prepared hundreds of fabulous recipes. Sadly, when she was diagnosed with Alzheimer's disease and moved to a skilled nursing facility, she was no longer able to use that lifetime collection. So, Aunt Jane gathered up all of Aunt Anna's special recipes and placed them into the bag for safe keeping. She saved a few recipes that were special to her, and then, knowing how much I loved to cook, she generously gifted the remaining recipes to me.

When she presented them to me, I felt as though I had also received a gift of the love that went along with each of those treasured recipes. Most of them were hand written on old index cards that had yellowed with age. By looking at them, you could tell which ones were well-used and loved, as they had food splotches and splatters on them from their frequent use in the kitchen. Some also included the dates on which they were prepared, as well as a 'review' of their flavor. It was such fun to imagine how they were shared and enjoyed by countless church friends and family members!

This recipe collection had grown over the decades, by collecting recipes from her family and friends. On the recipes shared by others, she credited them by writing their names on the top right corner of the recipe card. Virgie, Hazel, Iva, to name a few, had shared the best from their country kitchens. As Aunt Anna prepared these recipes, she also noted her own modifications out to the side. Like any good cook, Aunt Anna added her own personal touches and embellishments, even to the best of recipes.

With that sack of treasured recipes at home, I could not wait for my corporate day to be over! Each night I would pour over the recipes, carefully reading each one, and setting aside the ones that sounded the best. After testing and tasting, it occurred to me that this collection needed to be shared with everyone -- in the form of a cookbook!

At first, my husband probably thought I was crazy, but knowing my passion for food and my love for cooking, he supported my idea, and together we decided that I would leave my corporate job to focus on writing a cookbook.

After months of testing, tasting and typing, the end result was my first cookbook, *Timeless Treasures*, a collection of 200 old-fashioned favorites from the 1950s, '60s and beyond. Okay. So I self-published a cookbook…now what do I do with it? I had not really thought beyond the printing, and had absolutely no idea where to begin with the marketing!

While writing that cookbook from home, I had been watching the KOTV-Channel 6 (CBS-Affiliate) Noon Show during my 'lunch hour'. On that program, there was a daily cooking segment in which invited guests shared recipes with the viewers. Guests in the 'Cooking Corner' ranged from restaurant chefs, to dietitians, and sometimes cookbook authors. Well, that gave me the idea to go out on a limb and see if they would allow me to share a recipe with their viewers, too. After considerable time and prayer, I finally mustered the courage to call the producer and talk to her. She immediately booked me to do the show -- I was excited and terrified all at the same time! TV? Me? No way! Too scary! With building nerves and tension I could not sleep well for the two weeks leading up to my scheduled appearance.

The producer had asked me if I would like to come into the studio to see how they shoot the live show. What a generous offer! I immediately agreed and went into the studio to see how things worked 'behind the scenes'. It was not as intimidating as I thought it would be, but only because the people there were so very nice, and made me feel very welcome. First I sat with the producer in the newsroom to see how they put together the script for the show. Then, as the Noon hour approached, I took a seat quietly in the studio and watched with amazement as the one-hour show seemed to fly right by! No one missed a beat! The professionals -- from the anchor to the photographers -- were all flawless. I felt like I was in very good hands there, and my nerves were quietly calmed by the experts around me.

We all visited for a while after the show, and soon I felt as though I was just coming in to cook for a few friends, instead of the countless thousands on the other side of that camera lens. It was comforting, and I looked forward to August 11, 2001, when I would make *'Fluffy Pie'* for my new friends!

When the day finally came, I got a little jittery again, but was instantly relieved when I went into the studio and saw the friendly faces there. The cooking demonstration went well, and once the bright red 'on air' light went dim I was breathing a sigh of relief and ready to serve pie. Let them eat pie! *Fluffy Pie!*

After the show was over, the producer came out from the main booth to compliment me on my segment, and of course, to get a slice of pie! She then asked me if I could return for another segment the following month. Gulp. There went the nerves again! But with each cooking segment I felt more comfortable, and it quickly became really fun to do 'live' television!

When cookbook sales began to increase, I realized that I needed to come up with a business name. For a brief time I also offered aprons that my Mom and I designed together, so I decided to name my business 'Apron Strings and Kitchen Things'. Well, in the 'dot-com' world we currently live in, that lengthy name turned out to be...way too lengthy! I tried and tried to come up with something else, but to no avail. Then, one day my husband lovingly exclaimed "You are always in the kitchen, Kimberley!" And...Bingo! It had a nice ring to it, so I decided "Kitchen Kimberley" was my new alias! Thanks, Terry! The name fits me, and it has stuck with me and everyone else, quite well over the years.

My second cookbook is a collection of old-fashioned sweets and treats, called *Sweet Treasures*. It features delicious cakes, pies, cookies, candies and other sweet treats for every season of baking. A portion of the proceeds from both of my *'Treasures'* cookbooks benefit the Alzheimer's Association to honor my late Great Aunt Anna.

Over the many years of 'playing with my food', I have developed countless recipes. That led to my third cookbook, *The Joy of Food*, a collection of my own kitchen creations. It is filled with a balance of both healthy recipes and decadent recipes, thus my kitchen advice —"Whether you're eating for nourishment, or eating for mood...don't miss out on *The Joy of Food!*" My cookbooks are currently all available through my website: www.kitchenkimberley.com

Honestly, I never imagined that I would do any more than that *one* cooking segment on television, but here I am, nine years and 4 cookbooks later, and I am still cooking for all my 'friends'! Over the years I have gone from doing 'live' in-studio segments to doing taped segments from my very own kitchen at home. Whether my segments are taped or 'live', I always consider it a privilege to be a guest on the Noon show!

Throughout the years I have had the opportunity to meet some very talented and interesting people, and I have also made some very special friends. It is a joy to meet people who love to cook, and I have met many great cooks over the years; some have even shared their recipes with me!

By now you may have noticed that I did not mention culinary school. Well, I have never attended a culinary school, or even a cooking class, although I have taught several of them over the years! I have always loved to 'play with my food', which led me to dive into self-teaching of all things culinary. Daily, I actively read cookbooks from cover to cover as though they are novels. I also watch a number of cooking shows on television – not the fluffy, cutesy ones, but the informative, creative ones from which I can actively learn. I see each new day as an opportunity to expand my knowledge, improve upon my kitchen skills, and best of all, to play with my food!

I truly enjoy creating unique and delicious foods for you to share with your family. Of course, one day I would love to build on my television experience and offer a half-hour cooking show so that I can share even more tips, techniques and fabulous foodie favorites with you, and the rest of the world. (If you know any network producers, please put in a good word for me!). Seriously. Connections are the key, to where I want to be! Until then, my hope is that I am somehow helping at least one family to create special memories through food, like the ones I have shared with you here.

This book is the result of many years of hard work, but all of it has been enjoyable work for me. I hope you will now enjoy each of these recipes, and that they will help you to create lasting memories around your own dinner table.

Finally, please allow me to give you a quick 'pep talk' if you don't mind. Do you have a dream for yourself? I want to encourage you to always follow your dreams, and to never doubt yourself! You can do anything you want to do, and be anything you want to be! This world is limitless! No one can limit you unless you allow them to, and you certainly would never do that!

Go. Try. Do. Anything is possible, but you have to take that first step and be fearless about it! Each day provides a new opportunity, so please take it and run with it, as far as your dreams can reach! Never give up. There will be plenty of 'nay-sayers' and rejection on the path to your success, but do not allow that to discourage you in any way. Press on toward your goal, no matter how difficult that may seem. Encourage yourself! You can do it!

Thanks! I am now your official 'personal cheerleader'! My pep talk will not apply to everyone, and some may think it sounds cliché, but if it helps just one person who really needs it, then it was certainly not a waste of space, time or energy. Thanks for listening!

Again, it is my sincere hope that these recipes will help you and your family to gather together and make great memories while savoring delicious food!

Enjoy these Fabulous Foodie Favorites, and remember…cook, eat, smile, repeat!

-Kitchen Kimberley

Quick confession: I am a seasonal foodie!

What does that mean, you ask? It means that just as I never wear white after Labor Day, I never eat watermelon in winter! Of course I miss the flavors of spring and summer produce from October to March...just as much as I miss my bathing suit and flip-flops – but you will never see me adorn those during a snow storm; it would be totally inappropriate! Especially since I believe that snow storms are meant for snuggling under a cozy blanket with a cup of hot cocoa in one hand and a gooey-warm chocolate chip cookie in the other! By the way, I love snow. For me, snow means baking. In fact, I get 'snow' excited when I see the first tiny flakes fall, that I run to the refrigerator and remove a full box of butter to soften so that I can bake batch after batch of cookies as the flakes get larger and the drifts get deeper. Yes, I love snow, for a variety of reasons, but especially for the baking ones.

Back to my confession: In my humble opinion, foods that are out of season are also out of flavor; it gets lost somewhere along the way while making its trip to my local grocery store from some sunny location half way around the world! I can almost see the big, burly semi-truck driver pulling off at the rest stop and saying to his load of strawberries "okay, flavor, this is as far as you go – get out here!" Okay, so that doesn't really happen, but you have to wonder where the flavor gets lost along the way, because it certainly does! As a proud seasonal foodie I look forward to enjoying a fresh, sweet watermelon as its juice slowly drips down my chin; I also look forward to wearing shorts on that day, but I will wait for it all until the appropriate time! I believe that in life everything has a reason and a season, and that could not be more apt than when it comes to food.

This seasonal fall and winter collection is just for you, so that you can enjoy being a seasonal foodie, too! These are the tried and true recipes that my family and I have enjoyed for years -- my personal favorites. The following chapters are packed with everything you could possibly want to cook, eat, and enjoy during the cool seasons. With a variety of soups, a plethora of pies (and everything in between), there is something for everyone! Best of all, these all include ingredients that are at their peak during the cool seasons.

Please consider this as your "go-to guide" for delicious home cooked foods to enjoy during the cool seasons of each and every year! Happy cooking and happy eating!

Fall and Winter Pantry Essentials:

Keep your pantry well-stocked with a variety of these essential ingredients, and your cool season cooking will be easier than ever!

Canned Beans, Vegetables and Broth: Stock up on these, as they are all essential for making quick soups, stews and vegetable side dishes.

Pasta, Rice and Dried Beans: These all make great meal 'extenders', and complement casseroles nicely. These pantry staples will last indefinitely as long as you store them in a cool, dry location.

Quick Mixes: By keeping plenty of quick mixes on hand such as cornbread and biscuits, you can easily whip up some bread to serve with your favorite soup or stew when you do not have time to make it from scratch. Also, pancake and waffle mixes make a quick and hearty breakfast on cold weekend mornings!

Need an oil change? Check your cooking oils for expiration dates, and make sure you have plenty of fresh vegetable or canola oil on hand for seasonal baking.

Spice it up! Store a variety of seasonal seasonings, such as dried leaf oregano, basil and bay leaves for flavoring soups and stews. Also, a good salt-free all-purpose seasoning, and an Italian seasoning blend are both great for baked or roasted meats, and for casseroles. Finally, check your chili powder supply, and make sure it still has plenty of flavor. Oh, and don't forget the cinnamon!

Instant Hot Cocoa, Cider and Tea: Cozy up to the cooler temperatures with a mug full of warmth! These are great to have on hand for unexpected guests, too. Treat yourself or someone special to a comforting cup of hot cocoa topped with a dollop of whipped cream and a few chocolate sprinkles. Serve cider with a fresh cinnamon stick for an extra special touch.

Winter Squash: These are not only plentiful during the cool seasons, but also packed with fresh flavor and nutrients! If you choose not to eat them right away, you can also use them in seasonal centerpieces. Fill a pretty ceramic bowl with a variety of colorful winter squash as well as decorative Indian corn and gourds. These can really add pizzazz to your seasonal décor! Best of all, when you are ready to enjoy the squash, they can be easily accessed, prepped and roasted or baked to perfection!

Nibbles and Sips

Nibbles and Sips:

Sure, I could have called this section 'Beverages and Appetizers', but I thought 'Nibbles and Sips' was much more fun to say!

Cappuccino Brunch Punch

Coffee and Cappuccino are two of my favorite warm drinks, but this chilled punch is now a new favorite treat as well! Whether you serve this punch at a brunch or at a holiday party, you will surely get requests for this festive and frothy recipe!

Ingredients:

½ c. granulated sugar
¼ c. instant coffee granules
1 c. boiling water
8 c. milk
1 qt. vanilla ice cream, softened
1 qt. chocolate ice cream, softened

Instructions:

1. In a small bowl, combine the sugar and the coffee granules; stir in boiling water until dissolved. Cover and refrigerate until well chilled.
2. Just before serving, pour coffee mixture into a 1-gallon punch bowl. Stir in milk.
3. Add scoops of ice cream, stirring until melted and frothy. Enjoy!

Yield: 16 servings

Kitchen Kimberley's Tips:

❖ For an easy variation, substitute coffee flavored ice cream for the chocolate ice cream. Enjoy your *'Coffee Brunch Punch'*!

❖ For a fun twist, scoop the ice cream into punch cups and simply pour the coffee mixture over the top. Now enjoy your *'Cappuccino Float'*!

Chocolate Chip Cheese Ball

Get the party started with a dessert cheese ball! This is always the first to be devoured at an appetizer party. The combination of chocolate and cream cheese with crunchy bits of toffee throughout is irresistible!

Ingredients:

1 (8 oz.) pkg. cream cheese, softened to room temperature
½ c. mini chocolate chips
¼ c. packed light brown sugar
½ tbsp. vanilla
½ c. toffee bits
¼ c. powdered sugar
½ c. chopped pecans, toasted

Instructions:

1. In a large bowl, combine all ingredients except pecans.
2. Shape mixture into a ball and roll evenly in the chopped pecans.
3. Cover and refrigerate until ready to serve.
4. Serve with chocolate wafers or graham cracker sticks. Enjoy!

Yield: 12 servings

Kitchen Kimberley's Tip:

❖ The variations on this recipe are endless! Try using chopped white chocolate instead of the mini chocolate chips, and roll the ball in toasted, chopped macadamia nuts. Get creative and experiment with different baking morsels. Go ahead, play with your food and enjoy the fabulous results!

Cinnamon Roasted Almonds

Every fair and festival features these irresistible almonds, but why wait until a foodie festival when you can easily make them at home? These simple treats also make a wonderful holiday or hostess gift when placed in a cellophane baggie!

Ingredients:

1 egg white
1 tsp. vanilla
3 c. whole almonds
½ c. packed dark brown sugar
½ c. granulated sugar
¼ tsp. salt
1 ½ tsp. ground cinnamon

Instructions:

1. Preheat oven to 250 degrees. Line a large baking sheet with parchment paper.
2. In a large mixing bowl, lightly beat the egg white until frothy but not stiff; stir in nuts until well coated.
3. In a separate bowl, mix the sugars, salt and cinnamon, and sprinkle over the nuts. Toss to coat, and spread evenly onto the parchment lined pan.
4. Bake for 1 hour and 15 minutes, stirring every 20 minutes, until golden. Allow to cool completely, and then store nuts in an airtight container.

Yield: 3 cups nuts

Kitchen Kimberley's Tips:

❖ This cinnamon coating is also delicious on whole cashews or pecans, or a mixture of nuts.

❖ Nuts will dry as they bake, and crisp as they cool. Enjoy!

Cranberry Christmas Punch

Every holiday party needs a refreshing beverage, and this one is also beautiful with its festive red color! Whether you are serving this for a brunch or for a formal evening gathering, this punch will put everyone in a party mood!

Ingredients:

1 (3 oz.) pkg. cherry or raspberry flavored gelatin
1 c. boiling water
1 (6 oz.) can frozen lemonade concentrate, thawed
3 c. cold water
1 qt. cranberry juice, well chilled
1 bottle ginger ale, or cranberry ginger ale, well chilled

Instructions:

1. In a large pitcher, dissolve gelatin in boiling water. Stir in the lemonade concentrate.
2. Add the cold water and the cranberry juice; stir to mix well.
3. Place ice cubes or an ice ring into a large punch bowl. Pour punch mixture over ice. Slowly add the chilled ginger ale. Serve and enjoy!

Yield: 20 servings

Kitchen Kimberley's Tips:

❖ Make the punch mixture (through step 2) up to one day ahead; cover and refrigerate until ready to serve. This makes party service easy!

❖ For a fruity variation, substitute Pineapple-Orange juice concentrate for the lemonade concentrate.

❖ If desired, add scoops of fruit flavored sherbet for a creamy concoction!

Cream Cheese and Veggie Bars

Whether you serve these for a football party, or take them to a potluck as an appetizer, they are sure to disappear quickly!

Ingredients:

2 (8 oz.) tubes crescent roll dough
¾ c. mayonnaise
2 (8 oz.) pkgs. cream cheese, softened
½ c. sour cream
1 pkg. Ranch style dressing mix
¾ c. chopped green pepper
¾ c. chopped radishes
¾ c. chopped cauliflower
¾ c. chopped broccoli
¾ c. chopped green onions
¾ c. chopped carrots
¾ c. grated Cheddar cheese

Instructions:

1. Preheat oven to 350 degrees.
2. Press the crescent roll dough into a well-greased half sheet pan (18 x 13 x 1-inch). Bake the dough for 7 to 8 minutes.
3. Meanwhile, in a mixing bowl, combine the mayonnaise, cream cheese, sour cream and dressing mix together well. Spread the mixture over the cooled crust.
4. Mix the chopped vegetables with the grated cheddar cheese and spread over the dressing mixture.
5. Cover and refrigerate for 3 to 4 hours; cut into bars and serve.

Yield: 12 to 16 servings, depending on size of bars

Kitchen Kimberley's Tips:

- ❖ Any combination of firm vegetables can be used for this recipe; substitute 4 ½ cups total of your favorite veggies!

- ❖ Use half of the recipe amounts for a standard quarter sheet pan.

Creamy Artichoke Dip

Here is a fabulous dip for all types of entertaining. Whether you serve it at a football party, or at an elegant holiday appetizer party, it will surely be a hit! For casual gatherings, serve it with pita wedges or simple crackers. Dress it up a bit more for fancier service with gourmet crackers or breadsticks.

Ingredients:

1 (8 oz.) block cream cheese, softened
1 (15 oz.) can artichoke hearts, drained, chopped
1 c. mayonnaise
1 c. shredded Parmesan cheese
¼ c. roasted red bell pepper, diced
1 tsp. garlic powder
2 tbsp. fresh chives, snipped
1 tbsp. minced dried onion

Instructions:

1. Preheat oven to 350 degrees.
2. In a large mixing bowl or food processor, combine all ingredients well.
3. Spread mixture into a shallow baking dish, such as a pie plate or quiche dish; sprinkle with additional Parmesan cheese, if desired.
4. Bake for 30 minutes, or until hot and bubbly.
5. Serve with bagel chips, crispy garlic toast, or lightly toasted pita wedges. Enjoy!

Yield: 3 cups

Kitchen Kimberley's Tips:

❖ For holiday entertaining, garnish this dish with additional snipped chives.

❖ Plan ahead and use a tiny star shaped cookie cutter to make 'star shaped' pieces of roasted or fresh red bell pepper for an extra special garnish and beautiful presentation. You can cut these early in the day and keep them in the refrigerator for a few hours; just before serving they will be ready to use as a garnish!

Fabulous Fruit Dips

These are two of my favorite fruit dips for fall and winter entertaining; they are simple to prepare, but hard to forget!

Caramel Apple Dip

Ingredients:

16 individually wrapped caramels, unwrapped
¼ c. water
1 (8 oz.) pkg. cream cheese, softened to room temperature
½ c. packed light brown sugar

Instructions:
1. In a glass mixing bowl, melt caramels with water in the microwave, stirring frequently.
2. In a medium bowl, cream together the cream cheese and sugar. Fold in the caramel mixture. Serve immediately with fresh apple slices. Enjoy!

■■

Luscious Lemon Fruit Dip

Ingredients:

1 (7 oz.) jar marshmallow cream
1 (8 oz.) ctn. lemon flavored yogurt
1 c. heavy whipping cream, whipped

Instructions:
1. In a mixing bowl, blend marshmallow cream with lemon yogurt; gently fold in the whipped cream.

Yield: Each recipe serves 8

Kitchen Kimberley's Tip:

❖ Make the *Luscious Lemon Fruit Dip* even easier by using 2 cups of frozen whipped topping instead of the heavy whipping cream.

Festive Fruit Wassail

Hot drinks are always a welcome treat when the cool breezes blow outside, and this spiced cider drink will warm your heart and soul! It is the perfect beverage to serve for festive parties. The sweet aroma will put everyone in the holiday mood!

Ingredients:

½ gallon apple cider
1 (46 oz.) can pineapple juice
2 c. orange juice
½ c. honey
2 or 3 cinnamon sticks
9 thick fresh orange slices, cut in half
Whole cloves

Instructions:

1. In a 3-quart saucepan, combine the apple cider, pineapple juice, orange juice, honey, and cinnamon sticks over medium heat; stir to blend well.
2. Simmer over medium heat, but do not boil.
3. Meanwhile, push whole cloves into the rind of the orange slices; add to wassail and simmer until ready to serve.
4. Serve hot, adding an orange slice to each cup or mug, if desired. Enjoy!

Yield: 16 servings

Kitchen Kimberley's Tip:

❖ When entertaining a large crowd, this warm drink is always a hit! If you need the space on your stove for other dishes, simply prepare this ahead of time and transfer the mixture to a large crock-pot for serving.

Ham and Cheese Sliders

These sandwiches are ideal to offer when hosting a party for the big game.   Serve these hot and fresh out of the oven, piled high on a platter...then watch them disappear! Experience has taught me to make a double batch of these sliders, because they go quickly!

Ingredients:

1 (12 oz.) pkg. Hawaiian sweet bread rolls
2 tbsp. prepared mustard
8 oz. shredded Mexican cheese blend
¼ c. crushed French Fried onions
½ lb. shaved deli ham
2 tbsp. butter, melted

Instructions:

1. Preheat oven to 350 degrees.
2. Slice sweet rolls in half horizontally, leaving them all attached.
3. Spread mustard over both sides of the cut bread, and place the bottom layer onto a baking sheet.
4. Place half of the shredded cheese over the bottom layer; sprinkle with French Fried onions.
5. Arrange ham slices evenly over onions, and top with remaining shredded cheese. Cover with top layer of bread; brush top of bread with melted butter.
6. Cover with foil and bake in preheated oven for 10 minutes, or until cheese is melted. Cut into individual sliders. Enjoy!

Yield: 12 sliders

Kitchen Kimberley's Tip:

❖ The variations on this recipe are endless! Try one of my favorites – Smoked Turkey with Mozzarella cheese, or Roast Beef and Swiss. You could also use flavored mustards to spice these up a bit!

Marinated Lemon Shrimp

Prep-ahead dishes are the best for entertaining, and this beautiful shrimp appetizer gets marinated overnight to enhance the flavors. Serve it on your prettiest platter!

Ingredients:

3 lb. cooked shrimp
2 c. small black olives
1 ½ c. fresh lemon juice
6 tbsp. white wine vinegar
¼ c. olive oil
2 lemons, thinly sliced
1 medium red onion, thinly sliced
5 cloves garlic, coarsely chopped
2 tbsp. dry mustard
¼ tsp. freshly ground black pepper
1 tbsp. kosher salt
½ tsp. turmeric

Instructions:

1. Toss all ingredients together in a large bowl; marinate overnight in refrigerator.
2. To serve, using a slotted spoon place the mixture in a pretty serving bowl or a platter lined with lettuce leaves. Serve with toothpicks. Enjoy!

Yield: 12 servings

Kitchen Kimberley's Tip:

❖ Shrimp are sold by their size, whether by actual number of shrimp per pound, or by name, such as jumbo shrimp. For this recipe, I prefer to use either extra large, or jumbo shrimp. Extra large are labeled 16-20 per pound, and jumbo are labeled 11 to 15 per pound. Purchase shrimp from a seafood shop if you can for best quality and flavor.

Mexican Hot Chocolate

Ay, que sabor! Este chocolate caliente me encanta! See? I really do speak Spanish, amigos! I translate, too! I said "What flavor! I love this hot chocolate!" In any language it is a warm, soothing treat with a hint of spice that is 'muy delicioso'!

Ingredients:

3 oz. unsweetened chocolate
½ c. granulated sugar
3 tbsp. instant espresso powder
1 tsp. ground cinnamon
½ tsp. ground nutmeg
¼ tsp. salt
1 ½ c. water
4 c. milk
Garnish: Freshly whipped cream, light dusting of ground cinnamon

Instructions:

1. In a large saucepan over low heat, combine all ingredients except milk; stir until chocolate is melted.
2. Heat to boiling; reduce heat and simmer 4 minutes, stirring constantly.
3. Stir in milk; heat over low heat, stirring occasionally. Whisk until foamy.
4. Serve piping hot with a dollop of whipped cream and a sprinkle of cinnamon. Enjoy!

Yield: 8 servings

Kitchen Kimberley's Tips:

❖ Instant espresso powder can be found at most grocery stores. If it is not available in your area, you may substitute instant coffee granules.

❖ Keep instant espresso powder on hand to add to all things chocolate! Even a boxed brownie mix becomes decadent with the addition of 1 teaspoon of instant espresso to the dry ingredients. Or, add a bit to your instant hot chocolate for a quick 'pick-me-up' in the morning!

Mulled Apple Juice

When the cool winds come sweeping down the plain, this drink is sure to warm you up in a hurry! The aromas are fabulous and make the whole house smell like the holidays. In the fall, I love to take a piping hot mug of this drink out onto the back deck and watch for migrating birds. Even though all I typically see are falling leaves, it is still a relaxing and delicious way to spend a fall afternoon!

Ingredients:

1 quart apple juice or cider
1 tsp. whole allspice
½ tsp. whole cloves
2 sticks cinnamon
6 thin lemon or orange slices

Instructions:

1. In a medium saucepan, combine all ingredients except lemon slices.
2. Cover and simmer over low heat for 20 minutes, or longer, for stronger flavor; strain to remove spices.
3. Place a lemon or orange slice in each mug, and pour hot liquid over top. Garnish with additional cinnamon sticks, if desired. Enjoy!

Yield: 6 (3/4 cup) servings

Kitchen Kimberley's Tips:

❖ For a large gathering, this recipe is easy to double; store leftovers in the refrigerator and simply reheat to serve.

❖ Make an easy spice bag by tying spices into a square of cheesecloth. Or, purchase ready-made spice bags at kitchen supply stores. Either way, having a spice bag makes it easier to remove the spices prior to serving.

Munchie Mix

Got the munchies? These treats are the perfect way to satisfy all your sweet and salty cravings! Serve this tasty snack for movie night, a football party or simply keep it on the kitchen countertop in a pretty glass jar for a convenient nibble!

Ingredients:

1 c. chocolate covered peanuts
1 c. raisins or dried cranberries
1 c. dried tropical fruit blend
1 c. yogurt covered raisins
1 c. whole almonds or cashews
1 c. roasted soy nuts
Optional: Add 1 c. candy coated milk chocolate pieces in seasonal colors

Instructions:

1. Combine all ingredients in a large mixing bowl. Store in an airtight container. Enjoy!

Yield: 6 cups

Kitchen Kimberley's Tips:

❖ Mix and match these ingredients to your own personal taste! Once you have your family's favorite blend perfected, why not give it as a gift? Place the mix into a glass canning jar or other decorative jar, and cut out a pretty circle of fabric to dress up the lid. Tie fabric on with a coordinating ribbon, or with twine, for a country look. This also makes a fun treat for a college student's care package, or for friends at the office.

❖ Another of our personal favorite mixes for fall is the simple combination of equal parts of dry roasted peanuts and candy corn. Every bite tastes just like a candy bar!

Pappy's Party Mix

My brother-in-law, Pappy, loves spicy food! Whether it is a snack mix like this one or his famous Carolina Pulled Pork, his motto is 'the spicier the food, the better'! So, this party mix is for all the spicy people in the world, including Pappy! Oh, and incidentally, Pappy would like for everyone to know that although he may currently live in Texas now, he is from Nebraska...and he is a Nebraska Husker, through and through! Yes, Pappy has a bold and fun personality, and so does this party mix!

Ingredients:

2 tbsp. unsalted butter
1 tsp. Worcestershire sauce
2 c. mixed unsalted nuts, such as peanuts, pecans, almonds, or macadamia nuts
½ c. oyster crackers or tiny pretzels
1 tbsp. sugar
1 tsp. kosher salt
½ tsp. cayenne pepper (more to taste)
½ tsp. ground cumin
½ tsp. dry mustard

Instructions:

1. Preheat oven to 325 degrees.
2. Place the butter and Worcestershire sauce into a 9 x 13-inch baking dish; place dish in the preheating oven until the butter is melted.
3. Remove the dish and swirl it around evenly to combine with the Worcestershire sauce.
4. Add the nuts, oyster crackers (or pretzels) and sugar and toss to coat evenly. Bake for 10 to 12 minutes or until nuts begin to brown, stirring them once to ensure even cooking.
5. Meanwhile, combine the salt, cayenne pepper, cumin and dry mustard. Remove the dish and sprinkle the spice mixture over the nut mixture; toss to coat with the spices.
6. Return mixture to the oven and toast for another 10 to 12 minutes, or until the spices are fragrant. Remove from the oven and cool slightly. Serve warm or at room temperature. Enjoy!

Yield: 2 ½ cups

❖ Not a fan of cayenne pepper? Use garlic powder or onion powder instead.

Quarterback Queso

A creamy queso with big, bold flavors, and plenty of meaty texture in every bite! This dip is hearty enough to satisfy the appetite of a quarterback – plus it is super easy to make! There is no chance of a fumble with this recipe in hand!

Ingredients:

1 lb. mild or spicy bulk sausage
1 medium red onion, diced
2 lbs. processed cheese product, cubed
1 (16 oz.) jar salsa
2 (4 oz.) cans diced green chiles

Instructions:

1. In a large non-stick skillet over medium-high heat, cook and crumble sausage with diced onion until sausage is no longer pink, and onion is tender; drain well.
2. Place all ingredients into a crock-pot. Cover and cook on low heat until melted and smooth, stirring occasionally.
3. Serve warm with your favorite tortilla chips for dipping. Enjoy!

Yield: 12 servings

Kitchen Kimberley's Tips:

- ❖ Adjust the spice level of this dip according to your taste by using mild, medium or hot salsa.

- ❖ Leftover *Quarterback Queso* is delicious when spooned over a breakfast burrito, or added to leftover rice. Also try it with cooked pasta spirals for a different twist!

Strawberry Cheese Ring

Hosting a large gathering can be much less stressful when you have great recipes like this one that can be made a day in advance and refrigerated. Serve this savory cheese ring on a large footed cake stand surrounded by rich, buttery crackers for everyone to enjoy! This marriage of salty and sweet is absolutely irresistible!

Ingredients:

16 oz. sharp Cheddar cheese, freshly grated
1 (3 oz.) pkg. cream cheese, softened
¾ c. mayonnaise
1 small onion, finely chopped
1 c. chopped pecans
½ tsp. garlic powder
Dash of Tabasco sauce
1 c. strawberry preserves

Instructions:

1. In a food processor or blender, combine all ingredients except preserves; mix thoroughly until creamy.
2. Spray a ring mold, tube pan or Bundt pan with non-stick vegetable cooking spray; press mixture into pan firmly.
3. Cover and refrigerate for 2 to 3 hours, or until firm.
4. Unmold onto serving platter or cake stand; fill center with strawberry preserves. Surround cheese ring with buttery crackers. Enjoy!

Yield: 12 servings

Kitchen Kimberley's Tips:

❖ Use the shredder attachment of your food processor to grate the cheese, and then switch to the S-shaped blade for processing cheese with all remaining ingredients.

❖ For a quick and easy appetizer, use the cheese ring mixture (without the preserves) to stuff celery sticks. Garnish with additional chopped nuts.

Sugar and Spice Pecans

My family has always loved pecans, and for as long back as I can remember we have been gathering up our own pecans from local pecan farms. One year, our neighbor had a bumper crop from her pecan trees in the yard; my Dad offered to rake her pecan leaves in exchange for keeping all the pecans we could find there. It was an all day job for me, my brother and my Dad, but it was well worth it; we enjoyed delicious paper shell pecans all year long! I guess you could say we really 'cleaned up'!

Ingredients:

1 c. granulated sugar
½ c. water
1 tsp. ground cinnamon
2 c. pecan halves
1 tsp. vanilla
Cooking spray

Instructions:

1. In a saucepan over medium heat, combine sugar, water and cinnamon.
2. Cook until sugar dissolves, stirring constantly, about 8 minutes.
3. Add pecans and vanilla; cook until all syrup is absorbed and pecans are coated, stirring constantly, about 12 minutes.
4. Spread pecan mixture onto a baking sheet coated with cooking spray.
5. Separate pecans into halves. Cool completely. Enjoy!

Yield: 2 cups

Kitchen Kimberley's Tips:

❖ Store these treats in an airtight container in a cool, dark place for up to one month, in the refrigerator for up to 3 months, or in the freezer for up to 8 months.

❖ Shelled pecans can be kept in the refrigerator for about 9 months, or in the freezer for up to 2 years. Keep them on hand for making treats like these!

Super Stuffed Mushrooms

Entertaining at home would not be complete without first serving a fabulous appetizer, and this one fills the bill! With a double nutty flavor from both the mushrooms and the pine nuts, you cannot go wrong! These are always a hit!

Ingredients:

1 lb. fresh whole button mushrooms
2 tbsp. olive oil
3 shallots, diced
2 cloves garlic, minced
½ c. pine nuts (pignoli)
2 c. fresh spinach, coarsely chopped
½ c. Gorgonzola cheese, crumbled
Dash nutmeg
Salt and freshly ground black pepper, to taste

Instructions:

1. Preheat oven to 375 degrees.
2. Clean mushrooms with a damp paper towel. Remove stems; discard or reserve for other use.
3. In a large skillet, heat olive oil over medium heat. Add diced shallots and cook until tender, about 4 minutes, stirring frequently.
4. Add garlic, pine nuts and spinach; stir and cook for one minute; season with dash of nutmeg and salt and black pepper to taste.
5. Remove from heat and allow mixture to cool slightly. Stir in Gorgonzola cheese, and then stuff mixture into mushroom caps.
6. Place stuffed mushrooms onto a foil-lined baking sheet (for easy clean up!), then drizzle very lightly with olive oil.
7. Bake for 10 to 12 minutes. Enjoy!

Yield: 8 servings

Kitchen Kimberley's Tip:

❖ Gorgonzola is a veined Italian blue cheese made from unskimmed cow's milk. It has a salty 'bite' to it, and may be an acquired taste for some people. If desired, substitute another cheese such as Parmesan or Swiss for milder flavor.

Supreme Spinach Dip

We have all heard that spinach is very good for us, but this recipe makes it taste very good, too! Serve this with your favorite crackers, crudités, or lightly toasted pita wedges. Even the kids will eat this spinach!

Ingredients:

2 (10 oz.) pkgs. frozen chopped spinach, thawed and squeezed dry
1 (10 ¾ oz.) can cream of potato soup
2 c. shredded Monterey Jack cheese
1 c. sour cream
½ c. grated Parmesan cheese
1 tsp. onion powder
½ tsp. garlic powder
½ tsp. freshly ground black pepper

Instructions:

1. Preheat oven to 325 degrees.
2. In a large mixing bowl, combine all of the ingredients; transfer mixture to a greased 11 x 7 x 2-inch baking dish.
3. Bake, uncovered, for 25 to 30 minutes, or until edges are lightly browned and bubbly. Enjoy!

Yield: 8 servings

Kitchen Kimberley's Tips:

❖ Thaw frozen spinach easily in the microwave, or if you have time, set the package into a bowl and refrigerate for 2 days to thaw completely.

❖ No cream of potato soup on hand? Cream of onion works great, too!

❖ Turn leftover dip into a saucy dinner by stirring it into hot, cooked pasta. Add a little pasta cooking water to thin the sauce to your desired consistency; top with grilled chicken or shrimp and you have *Supreme Spinach Pasta* to enjoy!

Tiny Cream Cheese Biscuits

Years ago I made a double batch of these for a holiday party, knowing good and well that people would love them! They sure did – these tiny treats were all devoured before I could even get one of them on my plate! Proceed with caution, as these may be addictive!

Ingredients:

1 (8 oz.) pkg. cream cheese
½ c. butter, softened
1 c. self-rising flour

Instructions:

1. Preheat oven to 400 degrees.
2. In a large mixing bowl, beat cream cheese and butter at medium speed of an electric mixer for 2 minutes or until creamy.
3. Gradually add flour, beating at low speed just until blended.
4. Spoon dough into ungreased miniature muffin pans, filling full. Bake for 15 minutes or until golden.
5. Serve immediately. Enjoy!

Yield: 6 servings

Kitchen Kimberley's Tips:

- ❖ Each batch makes 1 ½ dozen tiny biscuits, so it is a good idea to double the recipe for a party.

- ❖ Spice them up! Add herbs to your desired taste, such as dried leaf basil, oregano, or chives. It's okay…play with your food!

- ❖ 1 cup of self-rising flour can easily be made at home! Start with one cup of all-purpose flour, and simply add ½ tsp. of salt and 1 ½ tsp. baking powder.

Toffee Cappuccino Mix

This delicious and creamy mix helps me to start my day off right! The comforting, smooth flavor allows me to gradually ease into the morning, cup by delicious cup!

Ingredients:

1/3 c. English toffee bits (brickle bits)
1/3 c. instant coffee granules
1/3 c. instant non-fat dry milk powder
1/3 c. packed light brown sugar
1/3 c. packed dark brown sugar
1/3 c. Original flavor powdered coffee creamer
1/3 c. Vanilla Caramel flavor powdered coffee creamer

Instructions:

1. In a food processor, combine toffee bits and coffee granules; process until mixture becomes a fine powder. Add remaining ingredients and process again until smooth and fine powder.
2. Store in an airtight container. To serve, add 3 tablespoons mix to 1 cup of hot water. Enjoy!

Yield: Approximately 16 servings

Kitchen Kimberley's Tip:

❖ Make a large batch of *Toffee Cappuccino Mix* to give as gifts by using the following measurements; process the ingredients in batches. This amount will fill 12 (8 oz.) jelly jars. Remember to add a tag with the serving instructions!

  2 c. English toffee bits (brickle bits)
  2 c. instant coffee granules
  2 c. instant non-fat dry milk powder
  2 c. plus 1 tbsp. packed light brown sugar
  2 c. plus 1 tbsp. packed dark brown sugar
  2 c. plus 1 tbsp. original flavor powdered coffee creamer
  2 c. plus 1 tbsp. Vanilla Caramel flavor powdered coffee creamer

  To serve, add 3 tablespoons mix to 1 cup of hot water. Enjoy!

Touchdown Tamale Dip

If you have a food processor, you can whip this dip together during a time-out! Scoop up this flavor-packed dip with your favorite corn chips or tortilla chips and score big points with everyone!

Ingredients:

1 (15 oz.) can spicy beef tamales, drained
1 (16 oz.) can refried beans
1 (4 oz.) can diced green chiles, drained
1 (8 oz.) pkg. shredded Mexican-style cheese blend

Instructions:

1. Preheat oven to 350 degrees.
2. Place drained tamales into a medium mixing bowl and remove the paper wrappers; discard wrappers and mash the tamales using a large fork or a potato masher.
3. Stir in the refried beans, drained green chiles, and half of the shredded cheese blend; mix well.
4. Spray a shallow 1-quart baking dish with non-stick cooking spray. Transfer dip mixture to baking dish and top with remaining shredded cheese.
5. Bake, uncovered, for 20 to 25 minutes, or until hot and bubbly and cheese is melted. Enjoy!

Yield: 6 servings

Kitchen Kimberley's Tips:

❖ For a milder dip, try using regular beef tamales instead of spicy ones. Spice it up even more by using Jalapeno Pepper Jack cheese, or add jalapenos or cayenne pepper, to taste.

❖ This dip also makes a delicious filling for burritos or quesadillas.

Satisfying Salads

★★★

★★★

Satisfying Salads:

Apple Pecan Crunch Salad

My, oh my! As soon as apple season begins, this salad is on my dinner table frequently. This delicious concoction combines the freshness of both sweet and tart apples with a cool and creamy dressing that is sure to leave you wanting more!

Ingredients:

4 red-skinned apples, such as Jonathan or Red Rome, cored and chopped
4 green-skinned apples, such as Granny Smith, cored and chopped
1 tbsp. fresh lemon juice
3 celery stalks, chopped
1 c. pecans, toasted, chopped
¼ c. packed light brown sugar
½ c. sour cream
¼ c. plus 1 tbsp. mayonnaise
1/3 c. dark seedless raisins
½ c. heavy cream

Instructions:

1. Prepare the apples and place them into a large mixing bowl; add the lemon juice and toss lightly to coat apples.
2. Stir in the celery and pecans; toss until combined; set aside.
3. In a small mixing bowl, stir together the brown sugar, sour cream and mayonnaise. Fold in the raisins.
4. In a chilled mixing bowl, whip the cream until just stiff. Gently fold it into the sour cream mixture.
5. Pour mixture over the apples and toss lightly until the apples are coated.
6. Serve in a large bowl lined with lettuce, or on lettuce-lined individual salad plates. Enjoy!

Yield: 10 to 12 servings, depending on size of apples

Kitchen Kimberley's Tip:

❖ To save time, substitute 1 cup of prepared whipped topping for the whipped cream.

Apple, Walnut and Blue Cheese Salad

Perfect for entertaining, this 'restaurant-style' salad is a cinch to make at home!

Salad Ingredients:

12 c. torn slightly bitter greens, such as frisee, escarole, and/or endive
4 medium Golden Delicious apples, cored, thinly sliced
¾ c. chopped toasted walnuts
1 c. Maytag blue or Roquefort cheese, coarsely crumbled

Vinaigrette Ingredients:

¼ c. vegetable oil
¼ c. walnut oil
¼ c. cider vinegar
2 tbsp. finely chopped shallot
1 tbsp. honey Dijon mustard
½ tsp. freshly ground black pepper
¼ tsp. kosher salt
¼ tsp. apple pie spice

Salad and Vinaigrette Instructions:

1. In a small bowl, whisk all vinaigrette ingredients until well-blended. (Vinaigrette may be made up to 1 day ahead. Cover and refrigerate. Bring to room temperature and whisk before serving.)
2. In a large bowl, toss the salad greens with enough vinaigrette to lightly coat. Divide among 8 salad plates, mounding in centers. Arrange apple slices around greens. Sprinkle with walnuts and cheese; drizzle with remaining vinaigrette. Serve immediately. Enjoy!

Yield: 8 servings

Kitchen Kimberley's Tips:

❖ To toast walnuts, spread on a baking sheet; bake at 375 degrees for 7 to 10 minutes or until lightly browned.

❖ Dip apples in a mixture of 2 cups water and 2 tbsp. fresh citrus juice to prevent browning; lemon, orange or grapefruit juice can be used. Drain and dry apples with paper towel prior to using in salad.

Cashew and Apple Salad

Salty and sweet are perfectly paired in this simple and scrumptious salad. The combination of standard pantry ingredients and easy preparation make it a great potluck salad or last-minute luncheon dish. Remember, an apple a day keeps the doctor away!

Ingredients:

½ c. powdered sugar
¼ c. mayonnaise
1 tsp. vanilla
4 celery ribs, sliced
2 small Gala apples, chopped
1 c. salted cashews, coarsely chopped

Instructions:

1. In a mixing bowl, combine powdered sugar, mayonnaise and vanilla until smooth. Stir in remaining ingredients. Enjoy!

Yield: 4 servings

Kitchen Kimberley's Tips:

❖ Select apples that are firm, with even color, smooth skin and a green stem. Apples with a green stem have been picked recently, and have not been stored for long periods of time prior to shipping.

❖ Store apples in plastic bags in the refrigerator to keep them fresh and prevent further ripening. Apples stored this way in the refrigerator will stay crisp and fresh for up to six weeks.

❖ When apples are in season, I eat at least one every day! Most of the time, I enjoy them simply out of hand, with slices of extra-sharp cheddar cheese or peanut butter. When I was growing up, my friends and I enjoyed fresh apple slices smeared with a little Cheez Whiz! Yum...I miss those days!

Citrus Salad with Bacon and Red Onion

Perk up your taste buds with this fabulous blend of sour, salty, bitter and sweet!

Salad Ingredients:

4 c. packed mixed salad greens, torn
4 c. packed baby spinach leaves
2 large navel oranges, peeled, thinly sliced, halved
1/3 c. dried cranberries
1/3 c. thin red onion slices
6 slices bacon, cooked crisp, crumbled

Dressing Ingredients:

¾ c. orange juice
3 tbsp. balsamic vinegar
3 tbsp. grated orange peel
2 tsp. packed brown sugar
1 tsp. ground cumin
½ c. olive oil
Salt and freshly ground black pepper, to taste

Salad Instructions:

1. Arrange greens on a large serving platter, or in a serving bowl. Top with orange slices, dried cranberries, red onion, and bacon. Toss lightly, if desired.

Dressing Instructions:

1. Place the orange juice, vinegar, orange peel and cumin in a blender. Blend for a few seconds. While the motor is running, slowly add the olive oil in a small, steady stream until mixture is emulsified. Season to taste with salt and pepper. Serve and enjoy!

Yield: 6 servings

Kitchen Kimberley's Tip:

❖ No time to prepare the oranges? Substitute 1 drained (11 oz.) can of mandarin oranges for the navel oranges.

Colorful Cranberry Salad

Whether served with ham, pork loin, or turkey, this salad makes a beautiful addition to the meal. The colors, textures and flavors are quite pleasing to the palate, and pretty on the plate!

Ingredients:

1 ½ c. dried cranberries
1 McIntosh apple, cored, chopped
1 Gala apple, cored, chopped
1 c. chopped celery
1 c. seedless green grapes, halved
1/3 c. golden raisins
½ c. coarsely chopped walnuts
2 tbsp. honey
¼ tsp. ground cinnamon
1 (6 oz.) container peach yogurt

Instructions:

1. In a mixing bowl, combine all ingredients.
2. Toss lightly to coat well.
3. Cover and chill for 2 hours prior to serving.
4. Stir, serve, and enjoy!

Yield: 8 servings

Kitchen Kimberley's Tips:

❖ To enhance flavor and add more delicate texture, plump the raisins and dried cranberries before adding them to the salad. Place them in a microwave safe bowl, and cover with liquid (water, orange juice, or pineapple juice). Heat for 1 to 2 minutes on high power and allow them to cool completely; drain them well before adding to the salad.

❖ Make a simple variation by changing the flavor of yogurt used in this salad. Vanilla, Strawberry, and Apple Pie flavored yogurt all make scrumptious variations.

Cranberry Fruit Salad

Everyone is always surprised when they learn that the star ingredient in this salad is canned cranberry sauce! Packed with such fresh citrus and fruity flavors, it is hard to believe that it is so easy to prepare. The combination of sweet and tart, plus creamy and crunchy is a real treat, and is also the perfect complement to roasted turkey or baked ham.

Ingredients:

1 (16 oz.) can whole berry cranberry sauce
1 (8 oz.) can crushed pineapple, drained
1 Granny Smith apple, cored and diced
1 Gala apple, cored and diced
1 Red Bartlett pear, cored and diced
1 large Navel orange
½ c. chopped nuts – pecans or walnuts

Instructions:

1. In a medium bowl, combine cranberry sauce, pineapple, apples and pear.
2. Grate about 1 teaspoon of the orange zest into the fruit salad, and then peel the orange, dice and add it to the salad.
3. Stir in the chopped nuts. Cover and chill until ready to serve. Enjoy!

Yield: 8 servings

Kitchen Kimberley's Tips:

❖ To make salad this more 'kid friendly', add a handful of mini marshmallows for a special treat.

❖ If extra guests show up for dinner and you need to 'stretch' this fruity salad, simply add two cups of prepared whipped topping to make it a creamy treat that will feed a crowd! Enjoy your *'Creamy Cranberry Fruit Salad'* and the beautiful rosy pink color that comes with the addition of the whipped topping!

❖ Toast the nuts for maximum flavor. This can be done easily in the microwave; heat nuts in a small bowl in 30 second intervals on high power until fragrant and toasted. Allow nuts to cool completely before adding them to the salad.

Cranberry Waldorf Salad

Here is a crisp and refreshing green salad that makes the most of seasonal fruits! Not only is it a new twist on an old favorite, but it also features the perfect balance of sour, salty, bitter and sweet in every delicious bite!

Ingredients:

6 c. mixed greens, torn
2 Red Delicious apples, diced
2 Anjou or Bartlett pears, diced
2 tbsp. fresh lemon juice
3 stalks celery, sliced diagonally
1 c. walnuts, toasted
1 c. crumbled Blue cheese
1 c. golden raisins
1 c. dried cranberries
Bottled Raspberry Vinaigrette, to taste

Instructions:

1. In a small bowl, toss diced apple and pear with lemon juice; set aside.
2. Arrange salad greens on serving platter, or in a large bowl.
3. Top with apples and pears   Sprinkle all remaining ingredients on top; toss lightly or leave as a 'composed' salad.
4. Serve with your favorite bottled Raspberry Vinaigrette, to taste. Enjoy!

Yield: 8 servings

Kitchen Kimberley's Tips:

❖ To toast walnuts, heat on full power in the microwave, stirring every 15 seconds until they are aromatic; allow nuts to cool, and then enjoy.

❖ Turn this into a main course salad by adding leftover roasted turkey. Slice or dice the turkey, and arrange over the top of the salad.

Favorite Pear Salads

Pear salads are a wonderful accompaniment to many fall and winter main dishes. I can remember many a meal of pork chops and pear salads...and here's the one I enjoyed as a child. Of course, we still enjoy it today, as well as my updated version, below. Whichever you choose, I hope you enjoy them as much as we do!

Mom's Pleasing Pear Salad for 4

Ingredients:

4 c. shredded Iceberg lettuce
1 (15 oz.) can pear halves in 100% juice, drained, juice reserved
2 c. shredded Sharp Cheddar cheese

Instructions:

1. Divide lettuce evenly among four salad plates. Top each with one pear half, and sprinkle each with ½ cup of the shredded cheese.
2. Drizzle each with about 1 tablespoon of the pear juice, to taste. Enjoy!

▪▪

Fresh Anjou Pear Salad for 4

Ingredients:

4 c. mixed salad greens
2 green Anjou pears, diced
2 red Anjou pears, diced
Juice of 1 fresh lemon
Extra-virgin olive oil
Crumbled goat cheese, to taste
1 c. toasted walnuts
Kosher salt and freshly ground black pepper, to taste

Instructions:

1. Divide mixed greens evenly among four salad plates. Top evenly with diced pears, then squeeze lemon juice over top; drizzle with olive oil to taste.
2. Sprinkle crumbled goat cheese and walnuts evenly over salads. Season to taste with salt and pepper. Enjoy!

Favorite Homemade Salad Dressings

Making homemade salad dressing may sound intimidating, but once you try it, you will be hooked! No more bottled dressings after a taste of these simple recipes!

Caesar Salad Dressing

Ingredients:

¾ c. mayonnaise
¼ c. olive oil
¼ c. shredded Parmesan cheese
4 cloves garlic, chopped
1 tsp. anchovy paste, or 4 minced anchovy fillets
1 tsp. Worcestershire sauce
1 tsp. Dijon mustard
1 tbsp. fresh lemon juice
Salt and freshly ground black pepper, to taste

See instructions below!

■■

Italian Herb Salad Dressing

Ingredients:

½ c. mayonnaise
1/3 c. white wine vinegar
1 tsp. canola oil
2 tbsp. light corn syrup
2 tbsp. shredded Parmesan cheese
2 tbsp. shredded Romano cheese
¼ tsp. garlic salt
½ tsp. Italian seasoning
½ tsp. dried leaf parsley
1 tbsp. fresh lemon juice

Instructions for both salad dressings:

1. Combine all ingredients in a food processor or blender until smooth. Enjoy over lettuce or pasta, or both!

Leafy Greens with Tangerines

Fun to say, but even more fun to eat – this is a salad you will surely make over and over again!

Salad Ingredients:

6 c. green leaf or romaine lettuce, torn
1 small head radicchio, thinly sliced
2 heads Belgian endive, sliced
1 small red onion, thinly sliced
4 Pixie tangerines, peeled, sectioned
1 c. honey roasted sliced almonds
½ c. crumbled Feta cheese

Salad Instructions:

1. Layer salad ingredients in the order listed, either on a large serving platter or in a pretty salad bowl.

Dressing Ingredients:

¼ c. balsamic vinegar
2 tbsp. honey
Juice of 1 Pixie tangerine
¼ c. extra-virgin olive oil
Dash of salt and pepper

Dressing Instructions:

1. In a mixing bowl, whisk together the vinegar, honey and tangerine juice.
2. Slowly whisk in the olive oil in a thin stream to emulsify; season to taste with salt and freshly ground black pepper.
3. Pour dressing over salad just prior to serving. Enjoy!

Yield: 8 servings

Kitchen Kimberley's Tip:

❖ Seedless, sweet, juicy Pixie tangerines are my all-time favorite citrus fruit! Look for them to arrive in your local grocery store in late winter; if they are not available, substitute Clementine tangerines or sweet navel oranges for this recipe.

Pear Salad with Sugared Walnuts

With the perfect blend of sweet and tart, and a beautiful balance of crunchy and creamy, this gorgeous salad is a dinner party favorite! Makes 8 yummy servings!

Salad Ingredients:

2 tbsp. unsalted butter
2 c. walnut halves
¼ c. granulated sugar
2 Red Anjou pears, thinly sliced
2 Green Anjou pears, thinly sliced
1 tsp. fresh lemon juice
4 c. baby spinach leaves
4 c. red leaf lettuce, torn
4 oz. Asiago cheese, shaved
1 c. dried cranberries

Salad Instructions:

1. For sugared walnuts, melt butter in a large skillet over medium-high heat. Add walnuts, stir to coat with butter, and cook for about 3 minutes, stirring frequently; add sugar; cook 5 to 7 minutes, stirring constantly.
2. Remove from heat; continue stirring until walnuts are nicely coated.
3. Transfer walnuts to a parchment lined baking sheet to cool completely.
4. For salad, toss pears in lemon juice to prevent browning. Arrange greens on a serving platter and top with pears and cheese. Sprinkle with cranberries and sugared walnuts. Drizzle with dressing just prior to serving. Enjoy!

Dressing Ingredients:

½ c. canola oil
½ c. raspberry balsamic vinegar
¼ c. granulated sugar
1 tsp. honey
1 tsp. Dijon mustard
1/ 4 tsp. ground black pepper

Dressing Instructions:

1. In a jar with a tight fitting lid, combine all dressing ingredients; shake well. Chill dressing until ready to serve; shake well again.

Sally's Pistachio Salad

Years ago, this salad was known as 'Watergate Salad', but today we simply call it 'Pistachio Salad'. My sister's Mother-in-law shared this recipe with our Mom, and every year since then it has been a sweet pairing with our holiday ham or turkey. This is one of those dishes that you can make a day or two ahead, as it holds well in the refrigerator. Best of all, it is easy to prepare...my brother even makes this one!

Ingredients:

1 (3.4 oz.) pkg. instant pistachio pudding mix
1 (16 oz.) can crushed pineapple
½ c. chopped pecans
1 (8 oz.) container whipped topping
¼ c. maraschino cherries, coarsely chopped
1 c. mini marshmallows
½ c. chopped dates (optional)

Instructions:

1. In a large bowl, stir together the whipped topping and the instant pudding mix, blending very well.
2. Add remaining ingredients (see tips!) and chill for several hours prior to serving. Enjoy!

Yield: 8 servings

Kitchen Kimberley's Tips:

❖ If making this dish a day or two ahead, add the maraschino cherries just before you are ready to serve.

❖ For a thicker consistency, drain and reserve some or all of the pineapple juice prior to adding pineapple to the mixture; add more juice to achieve the desired consistency.

Winter Greens with Warm Citrus Dressing

If it is true that we 'eat with our eyes first', then this salad is a fabulous feast for the eyes! It is a flavorful celebration of winter's best produce topped with a tangy citrus dressing that will wake up your taste buds!

Salad Ingredients:

8 c. torn assorted lettuce, including red leaf and romaine
2 heads Belgian endive, trimmed, sliced
1 small head radicchio, thinly sliced
2 pink grapefruits, peeled, sectioned
1 c. golden raisins
½ c. sliced almonds

Dressing Ingredients:

½ c. pink grapefruit juice
2 tbsp. balsamic vinegar
¼ tsp. kosher salt
2 cloves garlic, minced
2 tbsp. olive oil

Salad and Dressing Instructions:

1. Arrange the lettuce and the endive either in a large bowl, or on a pretty serving platter; set aside.
2. To prepare dressing, combine the grapefruit juice, vinegar and salt in a 2-cup measure; set aside.
3. In a small skillet over medium heat, dry toast the almonds for a few minutes until they are lightly browned; remove to a bowl to cool.
4. In the same skillet, add the olive oil and sauté the garlic until golden. Remove from heat, and let the oil cool to lukewarm.
5. Strain the oil into the grapefruit mixture and discard the garlic.
6. Arrange the grapefruit sections over the greens; sprinkle with golden raisins and toasted almonds.
7. Pour the warm salad dressing over, toss and serve.

Yield: 8 servings

Kitchen Kimberley's Tip:

❖ Not a fan of grapefruit? Substitute sweet Navel oranges and orange juice!

★★★

Soups:

★★★

Savor the flavor!

★★★

Soups to Savor:

All-Day Beef Stew

Crock pots can be a home-cooks best friend, especially when it comes to slow-cooked favorites like beef stew. The longer the flavors simmer together, the better they get; as a bonus, the aromas that fill up the house are yummy, too!

Ingredients:

1 lb. lean beef stew meat, cut into 1-inch cubes
1 white onion, coarsely chopped
1 lb. Yukon gold potatoes, coarsely chopped
4 celery ribs, diced
3 carrots, diced
2 cloves garlic, minced
1 ½ tsp. dried leaf basil
½ tsp. dried leaf oregano
½ tsp. dried thyme
1 bay leaf
2 tbsp. packed light brown sugar
2 tsp. Worcestershire sauce
3 c. beef broth
1 (10 ¾ oz.) can tomato puree
¾ tsp. kosher salt
½ tsp. freshly ground black pepper

Roux: 2 tbsp. butter and 2 tablespoons all-purpose flour

Instructions:

1. Combine all ingredients except roux in a 5-quart crock pot; cover and cook on low setting for 6 to 8 hours, or on high setting for 3 to 4 hours.
2. About 30 minutes before the stew is done, prepare the roux by melting the butter; this can be done easily in a small bowl in the microwave. Blend the all-purpose flour into the melted butter, stirring until the mixture is smooth. Add the mixture into the stew, and simmer for 30 minutes to allow juices to thicken. Remove bay leaf from stew; serve and enjoy!

Yield: 8 servings

Kitchen Kimberley's Tip:

❖ Serve with a big pan of cornbread for a complete and hearty meal!

Bacon and Black Eyed Pea Soup

What a delicious way to start off the New Year! We enjoy a steaming bowl of this 'lucky' soup annually on New Year's Day. If you turn your nose up to black eyed peas, please remember that the addition of bacon makes everything scrumptious!

Ingredients:

1 lb. hickory smoked bacon, diced
1 c. chopped celery
1 c. chopped onion
1 c. chopped green pepper
2 (16 oz.) cans black eyed peas, rinsed and drained
2 c. beef broth
1 (14.5 oz.) can stewed tomatoes
1 (14.5 oz.) can crushed tomatoes
1 tsp. Worcestershire sauce
Freshly ground black pepper, to taste

Instructions:

1. In a large saucepan over medium heat, cook diced bacon until crisp. Using a slotted spoon, remove bacon and place onto paper towels to drain.
2. Remove all but 2 tablespoons of the bacon drippings from pan. Raise heat to medium-high, and sauté celery, onion and green pepper in drippings until tender.
3. Add all remaining ingredients and bring to a boil; reduce heat and simmer, uncovered, for 15 minutes.
4. Stir in bacon and serve. Enjoy!

Yield: 8 servings

Kitchen Kimberley's Tips:

❖ Garnish with a dollop of sour cream, and additional crumbled bacon, if desired.

❖ This hearty soup is best when served with a pan of warm cornbread...yum!

Buffalo Chili

Good quality buffalo meat is the key to giving this recipe the best flavor it can possibly have! Of course, you can substitute ground beef, but the buffalo meat really makes this chili lean and mean!

Ingredients:

2 lbs. ground buffalo (bison)
1 medium yellow onion, chopped
4 cloves garlic, minced
1 (28 oz.) can diced tomatoes
1 (31 oz.) can chili beans
1 (15 oz.) can black beans, drained
1 (15 oz.) can tomato sauce
1 ½ tbsp. paprika
3 tbsp. chili powder
2 tsp. ground cumin
1 tsp. kosher salt
½ tsp. cayenne pepper (or more to taste)

Instructions:

1. In a large skillet, brown ground buffalo with chopped onion until meat is no longer pink.
2. Stir in garlic, cook and stir one additional minute.
3. Transfer meat mixture to a 6-quart crock-pot. Add all remaining ingredients; stir to combine well.
4. Cover and cook on low heat for 2 to 3 hours. Enjoy!

Yield: 8 servings

Kitchen Kimberley's Tips:

❖ Serve this chili with corn chips or tortilla chips, and/or topped with shredded cheddar cheese.

❖ This recipe can also be made in a large pot on the stove, instead of in the crock-pot. Just simmer it gently, uncovered, for about one hour, or until desired consistency.

Butternut Squash Soup

When the first cool breeze of fall air arrives, this recipe immediately comes to mind – it is my very favorite soup! A friendly viewer shared this recipe with me many years ago, and my family has enjoyed it countless times since then. This soup really hits the spot when served with a hearty loaf of fresh bread!

Ingredients:

2 tbsp. butter
1 large onion, chopped
¼ tsp. ground cinnamon
¼ tsp. ground cumin
4 ¼ lb. butternut squash, peeled, seeded, and cut into 1-inch cubes
4 ¼ c. chicken broth
1 Gala apple, peeled, cored, and diced
¼ c. apple juice

Instructions:

1. Melt butter in a large pot over medium-high heat. Add onion and spices; sauté 5 minutes.
2. Add squash, broth, apple and apple juice; bring to a boil.
3. Reduce heat, and simmer, uncovered, until squash and apples are tender, approximately 30 minutes. Allow to cool slightly.
4. Working in batches, puree soup in food processor or blender, or use an immersion blender. When soup is smooth, return to pot to reheat.
5. Season to taste with salt and pepper, and thin with extra chicken broth if desired.
6. Serve with a dollop of sour cream and garnish with chives or toasted squash seeds. Enjoy!

Yield: 8 servings

Kitchen Kimberley's Tip:

❖ To safely peel a butternut squash, pierce the outside with a fork several times and then microwave the whole squash on high-power for about 5 minutes. When cool enough to handle, it will be easy to peel!

Caramelized Onion and Sweet Potato Bisque

Luscious and creamy, this soup can be considered dinner in a bowl! The hearty and aromatic ingredients are sure to warm you up on a chilly evening!

Ingredients:

½ c. unsalted butter
5 large sweet onions, halved, thinly sliced (about 16 cups)
2 tbsp. packed light brown sugar
2 ½ lb. sweet potatoes, peeled, cubed
8 c. low-sodium chicken broth
2 tbsp. dry sherry or additional chicken broth
½ tsp. ground allspice
½ tsp. dried thyme
½ tsp. salt
½ tsp. ground white pepper

Instructions:

1. Melt butter in a large pot or Dutch oven over medium heat. Add onions and brown sugar. Increase heat to medium-high; cook 35 to 40 minutes or until onions are golden brown, stirring frequently.
2. Add all remaining ingredients. Cook 20 to 25 minutes or until sweet potatoes are tender, stirring occasionally.
3. Place soup in blender in batches, or blend until smooth using an immersion blender. Be very careful when blending hot liquids!
4. Return blended soup to pot; heat until hot. Enjoy!

Yield: 8 servings

Kitchen Kimberley's Tips:

❖ Select sweet potatoes that are smooth, firm and free of any blemishes.

❖ Peel sweet potatoes deeply enough to remove the hard layer beneath the skin; if not peeled properly, they will turn dark on the outside when cooked.

❖ Store sweet potatoes loosely in a cool, dark place, preferably between 55 and 65 degrees F.

Chicken Tortilla Soup

Years ago I created this soup after having a similar version at a restaurant. In order to make it easy and also to achieve the rich, creamy texture, I knew that I had to incorporate a condensed soup or two. So, I went to the soup aisle at the grocery store and dreamed up this idea based on what was readily available. It turned out great, and my family has enjoyed it ever since. It's one of my husband's favorites!

Ingredients:

1 tbsp. olive oil
1 lb. boneless, skinless chicken breast, diced
1 (11 oz.) can fiesta nacho cheese soup
1 (10 ¾ oz.) can cream of chicken soup
1 (14.5 oz.) can diced tomatoes with sweet onions
1 (15.25 oz.) can whole kernel sweet corn, drained
1 (4 oz.) can diced green chiles, drained
2 c. Mexican style shredded cheese blend, *divided use*
2 tbsp. chopped fresh cilantro
2 tbsp. tbsp. chopped fresh chives
Garnish: Yellow corn tortilla chips, freshly chopped cilantro or chives, diced onion, sour cream, or salsa

Instructions:

1. In a Dutch oven over medium-high heat, cook chicken in olive oil until lightly browned, about 5 minutes.
2. Stir in all canned ingredients; blend well and simmer for 10 minutes.
3. Stir in 1 cup of the shredded cheese and the fresh herbs; continue cooking for another 5 to 10 minutes or until cheese is melted and soup is heated through.
4. To serve, crush some tortilla chips into a bowl, sprinkle with a little of the shredded cheese, then ladle the hot soup over top. Garnish as desired, and enjoy!

Yield: 8 servings

Kitchen Kimberley's Tips:

❖ For a spicier version, add chili powder or cayenne pepper, to taste.

❖ Want more protein and fiber? Add a can of rinsed and drained black beans, pinto beans, or kidney beans in step 3.

Chunky Chicken Chili

A guilt-free version of chili really does exist – and it is scrumptious! The first time I tried this chili I was hooked, and so was my family. Use a rotisserie chicken from your local grocer to make this even easier to prepare. Yield: 8 generous servings

Ingredients:

1 ½ c. chopped white onion
1 c. chopped green bell pepper
3 jalapeno peppers, seeded and chopped
3 cloves garlic, minced
2 tbsp. chili powder
2 tsp. ground cumin
½ tsp. dried leaf oregano
1 c. water
½ tsp. ground red pepper
¼ tsp. black pepper
1 tbsp. Worcestershire sauce
1 tbsp. Dijon mustard
1 (14 ½ oz.) can stewed tomatoes
1 (13 ¾ oz.) can chicken broth
1 (12 oz.) can bottled chili sauce
4 c. bite-sized cooked chicken (white or dark meat)
1 (16 oz.) can Great Northern beans, rinsed and drained
Garnish: 1 ¼ c. each diced avocado and chopped red onion, ½ c. plain yogurt or fat-free sour cream

Instructions:

1. Coat a Dutch oven with cooking spray; place over medium heat until hot.
2. Add onion, bell peppers and jalapenos; sauté 5 minutes.
3. Add garlic, chili powder, cumin and oregano; cook and stir 2 minutes.
4. Stir in the next 8 ingredients (water through chili sauce); bring to a boil; cover, reduce heat and simmer 20 minutes.
5. Add chicken and beans, and cook 10 minutes or until heated through. Garnish as desired, and enjoy!

Kitchen Kimberley's Tip:

❖ Remember to wash your hands very well after handling jalapenos. For a spicy chili, include the seeds and membrane of the jalapeno; for milder flavor, leave them out.

Crab and Corn Chowder

Creamy, filling, rich, hearty, delicious...these are all words used to describe this comforting chowder. If you are not a fan of crab, be sure to see my tip below!

Ingredients:

6 slices bacon
2 celery ribs, diced
1 green bell pepper, diced
1 medium onion, diced
1 jalapeno pepper, seeded and diced
4 c. chicken broth
3 tbsp. all-purpose flour
3 c. frozen corn kernels, thawed
1 lb. fresh lump crabmeat, drained and picked over
1 c. whipping cream
¼ c. chopped fresh cilantro
½ tsp. salt
¼ tsp. freshly ground black pepper
Garnish: Oyster crackers, chopped fresh cilantro, crumbled bacon

Instructions:

1. In a Dutch oven over medium heat, cook bacon until crisp; remove bacon and drain on paper towels, reserving 2 tablespoons drippings in Dutch oven. Crumble bacon and set aside to use as garnish.
2. In the reserved drippings, sauté celery, green pepper, onion and jalapeno until tender, about 5 to 6 minutes.
3. Meanwhile, in a large bowl or measuring cup, whisk together the flour and chicken broth until smooth; add to vegetable mixture in pan.
4. Stir in corn. Bring to a boil; reduce heat and simmer, stirring occasionally for about 20 minutes.
5. Gently stir in the crabmeat, whipping cream, cilantro and seasonings. Cook 4 to 5 minutes, or until thoroughly heated. Garnish with oyster crackers, fresh cilantro and crumbled bacon. Enjoy!

Yield: 10 cups

Kitchen Kimberley's Tip:

❖ For a simple variation, substitute 1 pound of cooked, peeled shrimp, or chopped cooked chicken for the crabmeat.

Crock Pot Potato Soup

It is a wonderful and comforting feeling to come home to a big pot of homemade soup after a long day, and this crock pot recipe makes that easy to achieve. This creamy and flavorful potato soup will guarantee big smiles and full bellies for everyone in the family! Complete the meal by adding a tossed green salad and some crusty wholegrain bread.

Ingredients:

6 russet potatoes, peeled and cubed
2 leeks, washed and cut into bite-sized pieces
2 white onions, chopped
1 carrot, peeled and sliced
1 celery rib, sliced
1 tbsp. dried leaf parsley
5 c. chicken broth
1 tsp. kosher salt
Freshly ground black pepper, to taste
1/3 c. unsalted butter
1 (13 oz.) can evaporated milk
Garnish: Freshly chopped chives

Instructions:

1. Place all ingredients except evaporated milk and chives into a 4-quart crock pot.
2. Cover and cook on low for 8 to 10 hours or on high for 3 to 4 hours.
3. During last hour of cooking, stir in evaporated milk.
4. If desired, mash potatoes with a potato masher before serving.
5. Serve each bowl topped with freshly chopped chives.

Yield: 8 servings

Kitchen Kimberley's Tips:

❖ Reduce this recipe by half if you are using a 2-quart crock pot.

❖ Remember to wash leeks very well by cutting them lengthwise then rinsing under cold running water until all sandy debris is removed. With so many layers, it is very important to rinse them thoroughly.

Golden Potato Soup

This aromatic and flavorful soup practically cooks itself all day in the crock pot...what more could you ask for? Variations, of course! Several of them are listed just below the recipe. This soup is a chameleon so make it your own, and make it often!

Ingredients:

4 c. diced Yukon gold potatoes
2 c. diced white onion
2 c. baby carrots, cut into thirds
1 yellow or orange bell pepper, diced
4 c. chicken broth
1 (10 ¾ oz.) can cream of chicken with herbs soup
3 tbsp. butter
½ tsp. white pepper
¼ tsp. celery salt
¼ tsp. dried dill weed

Instructions:

1. Place all ingredients into a large crock pot.
2. Cook on high setting for 3 to 4 hours, or on low setting for 6 to 8 hours.
3. Enjoy this soup nice and chunky as is, or puree half of the soup in a blender or food processor. For a creamy soup, puree the soup in batches until smooth. Enjoy!

Yield: 10 servings

Kitchen Kimberley's Tips:

❖ Turn this recipe into *'Golden Potato Cheese Soup'* by adding cubed processed cheese (to taste) to the cooked soup. Allow cheese to melt, and then enjoy!

❖ Make this soup heartier by adding diced cooked ham or smoked sausage.

❖ Plain 'Cream of Chicken' soup may be used if the flavored one is not available in your area. Season to taste, if desired, with herbs you enjoy.

Ham and Lentil Soup

If you think you are not a fan of lentils, then you must try this soup! After the first bite, even the 'lentil-resistant' people I know have fallen deeply in love with the comforting flavors and rich, thick texture of this tasty concoction. It is a great way to use leftover holiday ham, too!

Ingredients:

1 ½ c. dried green lentils
1 c. chopped celery
1 c. chopped carrots
3 tsp. minced garlic
1 ½ c. diced cooked ham
2 tbsp. dried onion flakes
¾ tsp. dried leaf basil
¾ tsp. dried leaf thyme
1 bay leaf
¼ tsp. freshly ground black pepper
4 c. chicken broth
1 (28 oz.) can diced tomatoes with liquid
1 tbsp. balsamic vinegar
1 ham hock

Instructions:

1. Sort and rinse lentils well.
2. Place all ingredients into a 4-quart crock pot, stirring to combine well.
3. Cover and cook on low for 4 to 6 hours, or up to 8 hours if desired. (The longer it cooks, the thicker it gets!)
4. Remove bay leaf and ham hock prior to serving. Enjoy!

Yield: 8 to 10 servings

Kitchen Kimberley's Tips:

❖ Want to turn this into a vegetarian soup? Simply leave out the ham hock and the ham, and substitute vegetable broth for the chicken broth. Now, enjoy your *Lentil Vegetable Soup*!

❖ Green lentils hold their shape very well, and are best for long cooking methods like this one. You may also use brown lentils if green ones are not available.

Hearty Potato Minestrone

On a busy day, you can easily put this together in the morning and come home to a wonderful homemade soup for the whole family to enjoy. During the holidays, whether you are out shopping or at home decorating, it is a treat to have this hearty soup to look forward to for dinner. The aromas are simply fabulous, and the flavors...phenomenal!

Ingredients:

2 (14.5 oz.) cans chicken broth
1 (14.5 oz) can beef broth
1 (28 oz.) can crushed tomatoes
1 (16 oz.) kidney beans, rinsed and drained
1 (15 oz.) can garbanzo beans, rinsed and drained
2 c. frozen cubed hash brown potatoes, thawed
1 tbsp. dried minced onion
1 tbsp. dried parsley
1 tsp. salt
½ tsp. garlic powder
1 tsp. salt-free all-purpose seasoning
6 oz. fresh baby spinach
2 c. frozen peas and carrots, thawed

Instructions:

1. In a slow cooker or crock pot, combine all ingredients except fresh spinach, and peas and carrots. Cover and cook on low for 8 hours.
2. Stir in the spinach, peas and carrots and heat through, about 20 minutes. Enjoy!

Yield: 12 servings

Kitchen Kimberley's Tips:

- ❖ For a vegetarian version, simply substitute vegetable broth for the chicken and beef broth.

- ❖ Serve with crusty Italian bread and a Caesar salad for a complete Italian feast!

- ❖ This soup freezes very well. Remember to label and date all containers that go into the freezer!

Savory Meatball Soup

If your pantry and freezer are well stocked, then this soup can be on your dinner table tonight! These standard ingredients come together in a most unique and satisfying way. With meat, beans, vegetables and a savory broth, it will surely become a repeat recipe on your menu rotation. Makes 6 servings to enjoy!

Ingredients:

18 frozen meatballs (store-bought or homemade)
1 tsp. olive oil
1 c. diced onion
1 c. diced carrot
1 c. diced mushrooms
1 (15.5 oz.) can cannellini beans, drained and rinsed
3 c. beef broth
1 (14 ½ oz.) can Italian style stewed tomatoes
1 (8 oz.) can tomato sauce
½ tsp. dried leaf basil
½ tsp. dried leaf oregano
½ tsp. garlic powder
½ c. tiny shaped pasta, such as mini bow tie or ditalini
½ c. frozen spinach, thawed and drained

Instructions:

1. Place frozen meatballs in a microwave-safe dish and heat on 'high' power for 3 minutes; set aside.
2. Meanwhile, in a large (4-quart) pot, heat olive oil over high heat. Add onions and carrots; sauté for 5 minutes, or until onions are softened.
3. Stir in the mushrooms and continue cooking for 1 to 2 minutes.
4. Add meatballs, beans, broth, tomatoes, sauce and seasonings; bring mixture to a boil.
5. Stir dry pasta into boiling mixture; cover and cook for 7 minutes, or until pasta is tender; stir in thawed spinach, heat through.

Kitchen Kimberley's Tip:

❖ Keep frozen meatballs on hand for when you need a quick meal. They are great for a speedy spaghetti dinner, or for my favorite – meatball torpedo sandwiches! They can even be enjoyed as a party appetizer! Just simmer the meatballs in equal parts of barbecue sauce and apricot preserves or grape jelly. The combination of savory and sweet flavors is fabulous!

Skinny-Minny Minestrone

This recipe is as much fun to say as it is to eat! Personally, I like to make this as a Sunday night dinner for hubby and me, and then enjoy the leftovers for lunch during the week. It is scrumptious and super healthy – so dig in! Yield: 8 servings

Ingredients:

½ lb. lean ground beef
1 c. diced white onion
1 c. diced carrot
1 c. diced celery, with leafy tops
1 small zucchini, diced
3 cloves garlic, minced
2 (14 oz.) cans 99% fat-free beef broth
1 (10 ½ oz.) can beef consommé
1 (15 oz.) can cannellini beans, rinsed and drained
1 (16 oz.) can dark red kidney beans, rinsed and drained
1 (14.5 oz.) can diced tomatoes
3 oz. tomato paste
½ to ¾ c. uncooked small shaped pasta, such as ditalini
1 bay leaf
1 tsp. dried leaf oregano
1 tsp. dried leaf basil
½ tsp. dried parsley
2 c. shredded green cabbage
Freshly ground black pepper to taste

Instructions:

1. In a large stockpot over medium heat, cook and crumble ground beef until no longer pink.
2. Add diced onions, carrots, celery and zucchini; cook 10 minutes, or until vegetables are tender.
3. Raise heat to medium-high, and add all remaining ingredients, stirring well.
4. Cook, uncovered, until pasta is cooked 'al-dente', about 15 minutes.
5. Remove bay leaf, and enjoy!

Kitchen Kimberley's Tip:

❖ Not a fan of cabbage? Substitute fresh baby spinach for a colorful and tasty variation!

Smoked Sausage Stew

My husband absolutely loves smoked sausage, and when our grill is all covered up with snow and ice, this is a fabulous way to enjoy cooking it inside. A warm bowl of this savory, rich and filling stew only gets better when served with a hearty pan of cornbread. This one is a keeper!

Ingredients:

1 tsp. canola oil
1 (12 oz.) pkg. smoked sausage, diced
1 sweet yellow onion, diced
1 c. celery, diced
1 c. carrot, diced
4 cloves garlic, minced
1 lb. mini red potatoes, quartered
1 (14.5 oz.) can stewed tomatoes
1 medium yellow squash, diced
½ small head green cabbage, cut into small chunks
4 c. beef broth
1 tbsp. Worcestershire sauce
1 tbsp. paprika
1 tsp. dried leaf basil
1 tsp. dried leaf oregano
1 tsp. kosher salt
½ tsp. freshly ground black pepper

Instructions:

1. In a large pot or Dutch oven, heat oil over medium-high heat. Add smoked sausage and cook, stirring frequently until lightly browned.
2. Add onion, celery and carrots; sauté until tender, about 5 minutes.
3. Stir in garlic, and cook until fragrant, about 30 seconds, stirring constantly.
4. Add all remaining ingredients; bring to a boil, then reduce heat to simmer.
5. Cook, uncovered, stirring frequently for about 30 minutes. For a thicker stew, simmer longer, if desired. Enjoy!

Yield: 8 to 10 servings

South of the Border Pumpkin Soup

I love to "play with my food", and when it comes to creating this soup...I think I hit a homerun! With a flavorful blend of savory and slightly sweet ingredients, the whole family will enjoy this hearty soup. Oh, and the kids will never have to know how healthy it is for them...that will be our little secret!

Ingredients:

1 tsp. olive oil
1 tsp. unsalted butter
1 c. sweet yellow onion, coarsely chopped
1 (15 oz.) can pumpkin
1 (15 ½ oz.) can Cannellini beans
1 c. whole kernel corn
4 c. chicken broth
1 tsp. chili powder
½ tsp. garlic salt
½ tsp. ground cumin
½ tsp. Mexican oregano

Garnish: Mexican Crema, Queso Fresco and Multigrain Tortilla Chips

Instructions:

1. Heat olive oil and butter in a large soup pot over medium-low heat.
2. Add onion; cook until tender, stirring occasionally, about 5 minutes.
3. Stir in pumpkin, beans, corn, broth and seasonings; simmer 10 minutes.
4. Blend soup in batches using a blender until smooth; return to pot to reheat. Alternatively, use an immersion blender directly in the soup pot.
5. To serve, ladle soup into bowls and drizzle with Mexican crema; sprinkle with crumbled Queso Fresco and crushed tortilla chips. Enjoy!

Yield: 6 servings

Kitchen Kimberley's Tips:

❖ Cannellini beans are also sometimes labeled as 'white kidney' beans. They add both richness and nutty flavor to this delicious soup!

❖ Shop carefully when selecting canned pumpkin. Make sure you do not pick up the *Pumpkin Pie Filling* by accident, as the labels look quite similar!

Terrific Turkey Chili

There are countless variations on chili, and this turkey chili definitely ranks high on my list of favorites! Packed with lean protein and plenty of flavor, this is a filling and nutritious dinner that everyone will enjoy.

Ingredients:

1 tsp. canola oil
1 lb. ground white turkey
1 medium yellow onion, chopped
2 cloves garlic, minced
2 tbsp. chili powder
1 tbsp. dried leaf oregano
1 tbsp. dried leaf basil
1 tbsp. red wine vinegar
1 tsp. cumin
1 (15 oz.) can seasoned recipe black beans, with liquid
1 (15 oz.) can pinto beans, rinsed and drained
1 (8 oz.) can tomato sauce
2 (14.5 oz. each) cans petite diced tomatoes, with liquid

Instructions:

1. In a large stockpot over medium-high heat, brown ground turkey and onions in hot oil until onions are translucent and turkey is no longer pink.
2. Add garlic, cook and stir for one minute. Next add all seasonings and stir to blend well.
3. Finally, add all remaining ingredients, stir, and then reduce heat to simmer.
4. Cover and continue simmering for at least one hour to allow flavors to marry. Enjoy!

Yield: 8 servings

Kitchen Kimberley's Tip:

❖ Think spice is nice? Add a small (4 oz.) can of diced green chiles for more flavor and heat. Or, add cayenne pepper, to taste. Enjoy!

Texas Two-Step Taco Soup

My sister Sabrina who lives in Texas has been serving this delicious soup since 1994! As a busy executive, wife, Mother, and now Grandmother, she has relied upon this easy recipe to feed her family countless times. Her sisterly advice is to put your can opener in 'overdrive' and let it get a good workout. Two simple steps are all it takes to have a big pot of flavorful soup that the whole family will enjoy!

Ingredients:

1 lb. lean ground beef or ground turkey breast
1 medium onion, diced
1 (15 oz.) can whole kernel corn, drained
1 (15 oz.) can Ranch Style beans
1 (14.5 oz.) can diced tomatoes
1 (15 oz.) can pinto beans, drained and rinsed
1 (10 oz.) can diced tomatoes with green chiles
1 (0.7 oz.) pkg. Good Season's Italian Dressing mix
1 (1 oz.) pkg. Lawry's Taco Seasoning mix
1 can water – use more or less to personal taste

Garnish: shredded cheddar cheese, diced tomatoes, or a dollop of sour cream

Instructions:

1. In a large Dutch oven over medium-high heat, brown the ground meat with the onions and taco seasoning mix.
2. Add all remaining ingredients; reduce heat and simmer until flavors are well blended, about 30 minutes. Enjoy!

Yield: 12 servings

Kitchen Kimberley's Tips:

❖ Adjust the spicy flavor of this soup by using either a mild, original or hot version of the diced tomatoes with green chiles.

❖ If you really like spicy food, you could also add some diced jalapenos or cayenne pepper, to taste.

***

On the Side:

***

Perfect Pairings

for all your

Foodie Favorites!

***

On the Side:

Buttermilk and Bacon Mashed Potatoes

Creamy, dreamy...delicious! If you like potatoes, you will love this recipe!

Ingredients:

2 ½ lb. Yukon Gold potatoes, peeled, cut into 2-inch pieces
1 tbsp. plus 1 tsp. kosher salt, *divided use*
2 tsp. canola oil
4 oz. bacon, diced
2 c. lightly packed very coarsely chopped fresh parsley
½ c. hot water
1 c. chopped green onions
¾ c. buttermilk
¼ c. unsalted butter
¼ tsp. freshly ground black pepper

Instructions:

1. Preheat oven to 375 degrees. Butter a shallow 2 to 3 quart glass or ceramic baking dish.
2. Place potatoes in a large pot with enough cold water to cover; add 1 tablespoon of the salt. Bring to a boil over medium-high heat; boil 15 minutes or until tender. Drain potatoes and reserve pot for later use.
3. Meanwhile, heat oil in a large skillet over medium high heat until hot. Add bacon; cook until nearly crisp, stirring frequently. Pour off half of the drippings. Add parsley and hot water; cook 5 minutes or until liquid evaporates and parsley is tender. Add green onions; cook 30 seconds.
4. Place buttermilk, butter, remaining 1 teaspoon salt and pepper in same pot used to cook potatoes; bring to a simmer over medium heat. (Buttermilk will look curdled.) Add potatoes; mash with potato masher. Stir in parsley mixture.
5. Spread potatoes in baking dish, leaving top uneven so potato peaks brown.
6. Bake 30 minutes or until browned on edges and peaks. Enjoy!

Yield: 8 servings

Kitchen Kimberley's Tip:

❖ Potatoes can be prepared up to 1 day ahead through step 5. Cover and refrigerate. Bring dish to room temperature prior to baking, and increase baking time by 10 to 15 minutes. Love cheese? Add up to 1 cup of sharp Cheddar after mashing potatoes.

Butternut Squash Casserole

My very finicky nephew, Christopher, just loves this dish! For a guy who is typically 'anti-vegetable', he saves this dish to eat last because it tastes like dessert to him!

Ingredients:

2 c. cooked, mashed butternut squash
3 eggs, beaten
½ c. granulated sugar
½ c. milk
1/3 c. butter, melted
2 tbsp. flaked coconut
½ tsp. ground ginger
½ tsp. coconut flavoring

Instructions:

1. Preheat oven to 350 degrees.
2. In a large mixing bowl, combine all ingredients well.
3. Pour mixture into a well-greased 2-quart casserole dish.
4. Bake, uncovered, for 1 hour or until set.

Yield: 6 servings

Kitchen Kimberley's Tips:

❖ No coconut flavoring on hand? Substitute vanilla for delicious results!

❖ To prepare the butternut squash for mashing, cut it into cubes and boil just until tender.

❖ This recipe is also delicious when prepared with mashed cooked sweet potatoes instead of the butternut squash.

Christmas Rice

The festive colors in this dish make it perfect for the holidays, but the flavor will make you want to eat it year-round! This recipe was shared by a viewer many years ago, and I have made it countless times since then. I hope you enjoy it, too!

Ingredients:

1 c. long-grain white rice
2 (10 ½ oz.) cans condensed chicken with rice soup
1 ¼ c. water
1 tsp. kosher salt
2 large green bell peppers, chopped
1 large onion, chopped
½ stick butter, cut into pieces
1 small jar chopped pimientos, with liquid
4 oz. sliced mushrooms, fresh or canned

Instructions:

1. Preheat oven to 350 degrees.
2. In a large bowl, mix all ingredients together well.
3. Pour mixture into a buttered 2-quart casserole dish.
4. Bake, uncovered, for 45 minutes to 1 hour, stirring every 15 minutes. Fluff rice, and enjoy!

Yield: 6 servings

Kitchen Kimberley's Tips:

❖ For more color and flavor, use a mixture of red, green and yellow peppers. Also, add a handful of freshly chopped parsley just prior to serving.

❖ Prefer brown rice? Substitute some or all of the white rice for brown rice.

Corn Casserole in a Jiffy

Over the years I have made many versions of this casserole, but this one is our favorite. This comforting dish pairs nicely with everything from beef to pork. It is a standard dish on our holiday table, as well. This is a great potluck dish, too!

Ingredients:

2 (15 oz.) cans whole kernel corn, drained
1 (15 oz.) can cream-style corn
2 eggs, beaten
1 (8.5 oz.) box Jiffy corn muffin mix
½ c. unsalted butter, melted
1 c. sour cream (full fat, not light)
½ tsp. garlic powder
8 oz. shredded cheddar cheese

Instructions:

1. Preheat oven to 350 degrees.
2. In a large mixing bowl, combine all ingredients except cheese.
3. Spread mixture into a greased 9 x 13 x 2-inch baking dish; top with shredded cheese.
4.   Bake, uncovered, for 40 to 45 minutes, or until fully cooked in center.
5. Allow dish to cool for 5 minutes prior to serving. Enjoy!

Yield: 12 servings

Kitchen Kimberley's Tips:

*   ❖ With this recipe you are not limited to just whole kernel corn, you could also use a can of Mexican-style corn, or white corn.

*   ❖ Substitute 2 cups of frozen corn for the canned whole kernel corn, if desired.

Country Cornbread Dressing

Every Thanksgiving my Mom made this dressing for our family, and we still enjoy it today. For us, it would not feel like Thanksgiving without this comforting dish! We are thankful to have family traditions, but the special recipes that bind us together provide lasting memories of good times shared around the dinner table.

Ingredients:

½ c. unsalted butter
1 c. chopped onion
2 c. chopped celery
1 (9-inch) pan prepared cornbread
6 c. soft white bread cubes, crusts removed
2 to 2 ½ c. chicken broth
2 eggs, beaten
4 tsp. poultry seasoning
½ tsp. salt

Instructions:

1. Preheat oven to 325 degrees.
2. In a skillet over medium high heat, melt butter and sauté onion and celery until just tender.
3. Meanwhile, combine remaining ingredients in a large bowl.
4. Add sautéed vegetables with butter; toss lightly, mixing well.
5. Place mixture into a lightly greased 9 x 13 x 2-inch baking dish.
6. Cover with foil and bake for 45 minutes; remove foil and bake for an additional 15 minutes. Enjoy!

Yield: 12 servings

Kitchen Kimberley's Tips:

❖ Prefer to stuff the turkey? Lightly stuff the mixture into the body cavity and neck region of turkey. As a general rule, use ¾ cup of stuffing per pound of poultry. Extra stuffing can be cooked in a separate baking dish. Roast turkey according to standard roasting directions. To ensure food safety, the center of the stuffing inside turkey should be cooked to 165 degrees.

❖ For a variation, add 3 cups of sliced fresh mushrooms or 2 cups coarsely chopped apple and 1 cup of raisins.

Easy Gourmet Green Beans

When fresh green beans are not in season, this recipe makes the most of frozen ones! While I agree that fresh foods are best, frozen vegetables are processed at their peak ripeness – which is also when they are most nutrient-packed.

Ingredients:

2 tbsp. butter
1 tsp. balsamic vinegar
1 (16 oz.) pkg. frozen pearl onions, thawed
2 (16 oz.) pkgs. frozen petite whole green beans
¾ c. water
1 tsp. kosher salt
½ c. slivered almonds

Instructions:

1. Heat butter in a large skillet over medium-high heat. Add vinegar and onions; sauté until golden brown, about 5 to 7 minutes.
2. Add beans, water and salt. Turn heat to high; cover and cook until wisps of steam escape from around the lid; cook for 5 minutes longer.
3. Meanwhile, toast the almonds in a dry skillet, stirring constantly. As soon as they are golden brown and fragrant, remove them from the heat.
4. Serve green beans and onions topped with toasted almonds. Enjoy!

Yield: 8 servings

Kitchen Kimberley's Tips:

- ❖ If desired, substitute 2 pounds of fresh green beans for frozen; simply trim beans and snap into 2-inch pieces.

- ❖ Give this dish an Italian flair by adding one teaspoon each of garlic powder, dried leaf thyme and oregano in step 1.

- ❖ Stretch this dish by adding 2 cups of steamed tiny new red potatoes; simply toss them in just prior to serving. I grew up eating green beans with potatoes, and the flavors complement each other nicely! The addition of the 2 cups of potatoes will allow this dish to serve 12.

French Onion Potato Casserole

You may find the addition of French onion dip a bit odd in this recipe, but it provides a punch of delicious flavor, as well as creamy texture. Onion lovers will simply devour this casserole!

Ingredients:

6 c. red potatoes, diced, boiled until fork-tender
2 tbsp. unsalted butter, melted
½ c. whole milk
1 c. prepared French onion dip
1 c. grated cheddar cheese
½ c. French Fried onions

Garnish: Thinly sliced green onions, if desired

Instructions:

1. Preheat oven to 350 degrees.
2. Place cooked, drained potatoes into a large mixing bowl; smash potatoes, leaving some chunks for texture.
3. Add melted butter, milk and French onion dip. By hand, mash and blend well.
4. Transfer mixture to a lightly-greased shallow baking dish; bake, uncovered, for 20 minutes.
5. Remove from oven, and top with shredded cheese and French Fried onions; return to oven for 5 more minutes, just to melt the cheese and crisp the fried onions. Garnish with thinly sliced green onions, if desired. Enjoy!

Yield: 8 servings

Kitchen Kimberley's Tips:

❖ Personally, I prefer to leave the skin on the potatoes for added color, flavor, texture and nutrients.

❖ For a smoother casserole texture, use a mixer to whip the potatoes to your desired consistency.

❖ Yukon Gold potatoes work well in this dish, too.

Gorgonzola Mashed Potatoes

The bold flavor of Gorgonzola cheese comes through subtly when balanced with sweet cream and buttery potatoes! Pardon the pun, but after just one bite you will certainly be ready to 'whip up' these yummy potatoes again and again!

Ingredients:

2 lbs. Yukon Gold potatoes
2 tbsp. butter
½ pint heavy whipping cream
1/3 c. Gorgonzola cheese, crumbled
1 tsp. kosher salt
1 tsp. white pepper
¼ c. freshly snipped chives

Instructions:

1. Scrub and quarter potatoes; cook in a large pot of boiling water until tender, about 15 minutes.
2. Meanwhile, in a small saucepan heat butter, whipping cream, Gorgonzola, salt and white pepper over low to medium heat until warm, stirring frequently.
3. When potatoes are cooked to fork tender, drain them well, and return them to the pot.
4. Slowly add the warm cream mixture to the potatoes, mashing and blending well. Mash or whip potatoes to desired consistency, and then stir in the chives.
5. Taste and re-season with salt and pepper, if necessary. Enjoy!

Yield: 8 servings

Kitchen Kimberley's Tips:

❖ These potatoes are easy to make ahead! Simply spread the prepared potatoes into a 2-quart casserole dish, and then top with a few pats of butter; cover and refrigerate. When ready to serve, allow the dish to come to room temperature and reheat in a 250 degree oven for about 30 minutes. Stir well, and enjoy!

❖ Not a fan of Gorgonzola cheese? Substitute an equal amount of cream cheese.

Hominy Casserole

Hominy has been one of my favorite side dishes for as long as I can remember! When I was growing up, my Mom and I were the only ones who liked hominy, so we would share a whole can whenever she would make it for dinner! Today, I still enjoy the flavor of canned hominy, but especially when it is jazzed up in this delicious casserole filled with layer upon layer of fabulous southwest flavor!

Ingredients:

4 slices bacon, chopped
1 small sweet yellow onion, diced
1 green pepper, diced
1 clove garlic, minced
2 (15 oz.) cans golden hominy, drained
1 (10 ¾ oz.) can diced tomatoes with green chiles, drained
½ tsp. Worcestershire sauce
½ c. sour cream
Salt and freshly ground black pepper, to taste
2 c. grated cheddar cheese

Instructions:

1. Preheat oven to 350 degrees.
2. In a large skillet over medium heat, cook bacon until crisp; remove bacon using a slotted spoon to paper towels to drain.
3. Cook onion and green pepper in reserved bacon drippings until onion is golden brown, about 15 minutes.
4. Add garlic, cook and stir for 1 minute, then remove pan from heat.
5. Transfer mixture to a large mixing bowl. Add bacon, hominy, diced tomatoes with green chiles, Worcestershire sauce, sour cream, salt and pepper; stir to blend well.
6. Pour half of this mixture into a greased 1 ½ -quart baking dish; cover with 1 cup of the grated cheese, then repeat layers.
7. Bake, covered, for 25 to 30 minutes. Enjoy!

Yield: 6 servings

Kitchen Kimberley's Tip:

❖ Not a fan of hominy? Use two cans of whole kernel corn and enjoy your *'Southwest Corn Casserole'*!

Honey and Spice Acorn Squash

This old-fashioned favorite of mine is proof that great fall and winter squash does not need a lot of fussy preparation to taste fabulous! When the delicious aromas start filling your kitchen, you will count the minutes until this squash is ready to eat!

Ingredients:

3 acorn squash
¼ c. unsalted butter, melted
¼ tsp. cinnamon
½ tsp. salt
¼ tsp. ground ginger
1/3 c. honey

Instructions:

1. Preheat oven to 375 degrees.
2. Scrub squash well and cut in half lengthwise; remove the seeds and stringy fibers. (See tips!)
3. Place squash, cut side down, in a shallow baking pan.
4. Carefully surround squash with ½ -inch of hot water; bake, uncovered, for 30 minutes.
5. Meanwhile, combine remaining ingredients to make a honey sauce.
6. Turn squash cut side up, and pour honey sauce into cavities.
7. Bake for an additional 15 minutes, or until tender, basting frequently with sauce. Enjoy!

Yield: 6 servings

Kitchen Kimberley's Tips:

❖ For a simple and delicious variation, try this recipe using eggplant instead of squash.

❖ Toasted winter squash seeds are easy to make! Rinse 1 cup of squash seeds well and remove any stringy fibers; pat them dry and place into a small bowl. Drizzle with about 1 teaspoon of olive oil, and then season to taste, if desired. The seasoning can be as simple as a pinch of salt, or add herbs, cumin, or chili powder for a savory treat. Spread the seeds onto a baking sheet lined with parchment paper, and roast at 275 degrees for about 15 minutes. Cool on baking sheet, then enjoy!

Kimberley's Cornbread Dressing

For many years I worked to promote brand recognition and consumer loyalty for food products that are "Made in Oklahoma". I developed this recipe with that in mind; however I did not expect to create a new favorite dressing recipe for myself at the same time! If you can find local products, I encourage you to use them whenever possible. Help support your local farmers and food producers, and you will also help yourself to the freshest food for your family!

Ingredients:

1 lb. bulk breakfast sausage
½ c. butter
1 ½ c. diced onion
1 ½ c. diced celery
8 oz. sliced baby portabella mushrooms
½ c. roasted red bell pepper, chopped
½ tsp. kosher salt
4 tsp. poultry seasoning
½ tsp. dried leaf oregano
2 eggs, beaten
2 ½ c. chicken broth
2 (8.5 oz.) pkgs. cornbread mix, prepared, crumbled
6 c. soft bread cubes, crusts removed

Instructions:

1. Preheat oven to 325 degrees.
2. In a large skillet over medium-high heat, cook and crumble sausage until no longer pink.
3. Meanwhile, in another large skillet, melt butter; add onions and celery. Cook, stirring frequently until softened, about 10 minutes; add mushrooms to skillet, cook for an additional 5 minutes.
4. Transfer cooked sausage and vegetables to a large mixing bowl; add all remaining ingredients. Toss mixture lightly, blending well.
5. Spoon mixture into a greased 9 x 13 x 2-inch baking dish; cover with foil and bake for 45 minutes; uncover and bake for an additional 15 minutes. Enjoy!

Yield: 12 servings

Mexican Charro Beans

A Mexican feast at my house would not be complete without these tasty beans. They are quite similar to the ones we enjoy at our favorite Mexican restaurant!

Ingredients:

½ lb. bacon, diced
1 large yellow onion, diced
5 (16 oz.) cans pinto beans, rinsed and drained
1 (4 oz.) can diced green chiles
1 c. beef broth
¼ tsp. cayenne pepper, or more to taste
1 tsp. ground cumin
1 tsp. chili powder
2 cloves garlic, minced

Instructions:

1. In a Dutch oven over medium heat, fry bacon until crisp; remove to paper towels to drain.
2. In remaining bacon drippings, cook onion until light brown and tender.
3. Reserve 1 cup of the pinto beans, and add remaining beans to pot, along with all remaining ingredients.
4. Mash the reserved beans, and add then add them to the pot; stir well.
5. Reduce heat to low and simmer, uncovered, until beans become thick and soupy, about 30 minutes.
6. Stir in reserved bacon; heat 5 minutes longer. Enjoy!

Yield: 8 servings

Kitchen Kimberley's Tip:

❖ Got leftovers? Mash them well and heat thoroughly in a large non-stick skillet. This mixture is great for making bean burritos or bean quesadillas!

Mom's Spanish Rice

The aromas of this delicious rice remind me of when my parents would host our high school Spanish Club parties. My Mom quadrupled this recipe to serve 20 hungry teenagers, and there was never a grain of rice leftover! We still enjoy this flavorful recipe with every Mexican Fiesta!

Ingredients:

½ c. thinly sliced white onion
½ c. diced green pepper
2 c. instant white rice
¼ c. bacon drippings or butter
2 c. hot water
2 (8 oz.) cans tomato sauce
1 tsp. salt
Dash pepper

Instructions:

1. In a large skillet, sauté onion, green pepper and rice in the bacon drippings or butter.
2. Add remaining ingredients; mix well.
3. Bring to a boil, and then reduce heat and simmer, uncovered, for 5 minutes. Fluff rice, and serve. Enjoy!

Yield: 4 to 6 servings

Kitchen Kimberley's Tips:

❖ 'Beef up' this side dish by sautéing one pound of lean ground beef with the vegetable and rice mixture. Or, cook and crumble Mexican Chorizo first, drain well and then add the vegetables and rice.

❖ Got leftover rice? Add a can of rinsed and drained red beans to one cup of leftover rice for quick dish of *'Red Beans and Rice'*! Makes a great lunch!

❖ This dish makes a wonderful accompaniment to any steak, chicken or Mexican entrée.

Oven Roasted Sweet Potatoes & Onions

Rustic, cozy, comforting...these are all words that come to mind when I think of this simple, yet fabulous side dish. Roasting at a high temperature intensifies the sweetness of the vegetables, while the vinegar gives them a nice, tangy bite!

Ingredients:

2 lbs. sweet potatoes
1 large red onion
3 tbsp. olive oil
2 tbsp. balsamic vinegar
1 tsp. kosher salt
¼ tsp. garlic powder
¼ tsp. freshly ground black pepper
¼ tsp. dried leaf marjoram

Instructions:

1. Preheat oven to 425 degrees.
2. Scrub potatoes and cut into 1-inch pieces.
3. Peel and cut red onion into 1-inch pieces.
4. Place potatoes and onions on a large shallow baking sheet; drizzle with olive oil and balsamic vinegar; sprinkle with seasonings.
5. Toss lightly to coat well and evenly; spread vegetables into an even layer.
6. Roast for 40 minutes, stirring after 20 minutes. Enjoy!

Yield: 6 servings

Kitchen Kimberley's Tips:

❖ Leftover roasted vegetables can be whipped into a creamy and delicious soup! Simply place leftover vegetables in a blender and add warm chicken stock, one cup at a time, until desired consistency is achieved. Season to taste, and enjoy!

❖ Another great way to enjoy leftover roasted vegetables is as a filling for wrap sandwiches. Add store-bought hummus for protein, and you will have a hearty, and filling lunch-time treat!

Scalloped Carrot Casserole

Old-fashioned recipes like this one are hard to beat! The creamy cheese sauce is also delicious when served over steamed broccoli or cauliflower. I do love a recipe within a recipe, don't you? Hope you enjoy this old-fashioned family favorite!

Ingredients:

12 medium carrots, peeled, sliced
1 small onion, minced
¼ c. unsalted butter
¼ c. all-purpose flour
½ tsp. salt
¼ tsp. dry mustard
2 c. milk
1/8 tsp. freshly ground black pepper
¼ tsp. celery salt
1 (1 oz.) pkg. Ranch dressing mix
1 c. Cheez Whiz Original cheese dip

Instructions:

1. Preheat oven to 350 degrees.
2. In a large pot of boiling water cook carrots until tender; drain well and place carrots into a greased 3-quart baking dish.
3. Meanwhile, in a large saucepan over medium-high heat, melt butter and sauté onion until tender; whisk in flour, salt and dry mustard until smooth.
4. Add milk and cook until thick, stirring constantly.
5. Stir in remaining ingredients, whisking until smooth and creamy.
6. Pour sauce over carrots in casserole dish.
7. If desired, top with crushed buttery cracker crumbs or plain bread crumbs.
8. Bake, uncovered, for 30 minutes or until hot and bubbly. Enjoy!

Yield: 12 servings

Kitchen Kimberley's Tips:

❖ Modern-Day Method: Steam or boil 2 lbs. baby carrots until tender; proceed as directed. Enjoy your *'Baby Carrot Casserole'*!

❖ The cheese sauce can be served over any cooked vegetable, such as Brussels sprouts, broccoli, cauliflower, or even peas. Also, try stirring it into cooked pasta for another creamy side dish.

Southern Green Beans

This here recipe gives my Midwest mouth a Southern drawl, y'all! (Okay, now say that again with your best 'Su-thun' accent, and then laugh out loud!) Seriously, I do declare that some of the best food in the world comes from the American South, including these scrumptious green beans. Frankly, my dear...you must make this recipe, and enjoy every delicious Southern bite!

Ingredients:

3 slices peppered bacon, diced
3 shallots, sliced
3 cloves garlic, minced
3 tsp. balsamic vinegar
3 (14.5 oz) cans green beans, drained

Instructions:

1. In a large, deep skillet over medium-high heat, cook bacon until almost crisp.
2. Add shallot and garlic; cook and stir an additional 3 to 4 minutes.
3. Stir in balsamic vinegar and drained green beans.
4. Reduce heat to low, simmer 5 minutes, stirring occasionally. Enjoy!

Yield: 6 servings

Kitchen Kimberley's Tips:

❖ Find peppered bacon sold by the slice at the butcher counter, or simply use regular bacon and add freshly ground black pepper to your taste.

❖ Shallots have a mild onion flavor with a subtle hint of garlic. Prepare them just as you would an onion – simply peel and slice!

❖ Try this recipe with canned corn instead of green beans for another delicious side dish...*Southern Corn!*

Special Sweet Potato Casserole

This casserole combines 3 of my favorite holiday flavors--sweet potatoes, cranberries and pecans! Each and every bite is scrumptious! Yield: 8 servings

Casserole Ingredients:

5 large sweet potatoes, peeled and quartered
½ c. orange marmalade
½ c. butter pecan flavored syrup (pancake syrup)
1 Granny Smith apple, cored and diced
1 Bartlett pear, cored and diced
1 c. fresh cranberries
Juice of one fresh orange
½ c. packed dark brown sugar

Casserole Instructions:

1. In a large pot, boil sweet potatoes until fork tender; drain well. Return potatoes to pot and add orange marmalade and butter pecan syrup; mash well and spread mixture into a greased 2-quart casserole dish; set aside.
2. Meanwhile, in a saucepan over medium heat combine apple, pear, cranberries, orange juice and brown sugar; simmer for 20 minutes, or until fruit is tender and mixture is slightly thickened. Spread fruit mixture over the sweet potato mixture in casserole dish.
3. Prepare topping and preheat oven to 350 degrees.

Topping Ingredients:

1 c. packed dark brown sugar
1 c. all-purpose flour
½ c. chopped walnuts or pecans
½ c. old-fashioned oats
½ tsp. ground cinnamon
½ tsp. salt
½ c. butter, melted

Topping Instructions:

1. In a large mixing bowl, combine all dry ingredients. Stir in the melted butter, making sure that all ingredients are evenly moistened. Sprinkle topping over the fruit mixture, covering completely. Bake, uncovered, for 35 to 40 minutes or until topping is crispy and lightly browned. Enjoy!

Squash and Apple Bake

This dish combines two simple yet fabulous fall flavors -- butternut squash and apples -- and turns them into a tender and golden feast for the senses. Yes, this is a side dish, but you might just think you are eating dessert! Enjoy the complementary flavors of nutty squash, sweet-tart apples and brown sugar lightly kissed with fall spices in this comforting casserole.

Ingredients:

2 small butternut squash (about 2 lbs.)
2 Granny Smith apples, peeled, cored, and thinly sliced
½ c. packed dark brown sugar
¼ c. butter, melted and cooled
1 tbsp. all-purpose flour
1 tsp. salt
½ tsp. pumpkin pie spice

Instructions:

1. Preheat oven to 350 degrees.
2. To soften squash, microwave each one on high for 2 minutes. When cool enough to handle, peel squash and cut into ½-inch thick slices.
3. Arrange squash slices in a greased, shallow baking dish; top with apple slices.
4. In a small bowl, combine remaining ingredients well and spoon over apples and squash.
5. Cover dish tightly with foil, and bake for 1 hour, or until squash is tender. Enjoy!

Yield: 8 servings

Kitchen Kimberley's Tips:

❖ Melt the butter in the microwave in a glass measuring cup, and then add the remaining ingredients. Since glass measuring cups have a spout, it is easy to then pour the mixture over the apples and squash.

❖ For crunchy texture, top with 1 cup of chopped pecans during the last 10 minutes of baking.

Stuffing Casserole

It amazes me how such a short ingredient list can come together to create such comforting flavor! This is my favorite side dish for roasted chicken or Cornish hens, and it could not be quicker or easier to prepare! So simple...yet so scrumptious!

Ingredients:

8 oz. dry seasoned stuffing mix
1 (10 ¾ oz.) can cream of celery soup
1 (10 ¾ oz.) can cream of chicken soup
1 ¼ c. chicken broth
1 cup evaporated milk

Instructions:

1. Preheat oven to 350 degrees.
2. In a large mixing bowl, combine all ingredients well.
3. Spread mixture into a well-greased 9 x 13-inch baking dish.
4. Bake for 40 to 45 minutes. Enjoy!

Yield: 12 servings

Kitchen Kimberley's Tips:

❖ Leftovers can be used in a variety of ways! Try making one of my favorites – a *'Smothered Stuffing Sandwich'* made with slices of warmed leftover roasted chicken or turkey and a thin layer of stuffing casserole on a soft hoagie bun. Smother the whole sandwich with either chicken or turkey gravy, and enjoy this sandwich with a fork!

❖ Using this recipe makes my *'Stuffing Stuffed Mushrooms'* easy and delicious! Simply stuff a mushroom cap with spoonfuls of cooked *Stuffing Casserole*, place on a baking sheet, drizzle with a little olive oil or melted butter, and bake in a preheated 375-degree oven for about 10 minutes.

Sweet Peas with Cheese

Everyone knows that it is a challenge to get kids (and some adults!) to eat peas. When I was growing up, we always had 'creamed peas', which made them much easier to tolerate as a kid. Now, with the addition of cheddar cheese, and a spoonful of sugar, even the picky eaters will be asking for 'more Sweet Peas with Cheese, please'!

Ingredients:

2 tbsp. butter
1 clove minced garlic
2 tbsp. flour
1 tsp. granulated sugar
1 ½ c. milk
1 c. shredded cheddar cheese
Freshly ground black pepper, to taste
2 c. frozen sweet peas

Instructions:

1. In a large skillet over medium-high heat, melt butter; add garlic and cook for 1 minute, stirring constantly.
2. Add flour and sugar; cook for 1 minute, again stirring constantly.
3. Slowly add milk, whisking until smooth.
4. Add shredded cheese; stir until melted and smooth.
5. Season to taste with freshly ground black pepper.
6. Stir in frozen peas; reduce heat to medium and cook for 5 minutes, or just until peas are heated through to retain bright green color. Enjoy!

Yield: 4 servings

Kitchen Kimberley's Tips:

❖ Use a 10 oz. box of frozen sweet peas, or use two cups from a larger bag.

❖ Turn this side dish into a main course by adding one small can of drained albacore tuna and a small can of drained carrots in step 6. Serve this warm mixture over toasted wheat bread, and enjoy your *'Creamed Tuna fish on Toast'* – a classic dish I enjoyed countless times during my childhood.

Sweet Potatoes in Orange Cups

Want to impress your friends and family? There is no easier way than to prepare this flavorful sweet potato dish that is served in an orange 'cup'! It may sound super fancy, but it is simple to do, and absolutely gorgeous to serve for company!

Ingredients:

4 small navel oranges
2 c. cooked, mashed sweet potato
¼ c. firmly packed brown sugar
1 tsp. grated orange rind
¼ c. plus 2 tbsp. fresh orange juice
1 tsp. butter flavoring
¾ tsp. ground cinnamon
¼ tsp. salt
½ c. miniature marshmallows

Instructions:

1. Preheat oven to 350 degrees.
2. Cut oranges in half crosswise. Clip membranes and carefully remove pulp without puncturing bottom of orange. Reserve orange pulp for other uses.
3. In a large mixing bowl, combine sweet potato and next six ingredients; spoon mixture evenly into the prepared orange cups.
4. Carefully place filled cups into a 9-inch square baking pan.
5. Cover with foil and bake for 20 minutes or until thoroughly heated.
6. Remove foil and sprinkle with marshmallows; bake 5 minutes longer, or until marshmallows melt. Enjoy!

Yield: 4 servings

Kitchen Kimberley's Tips:

❖ Use the orange pulp to make my *Cranberry Fruit Salad* on page 50. The two recipes go beautifully together and are the perfect complement to baked ham, turkey, or pork roast.

❖ Nuts about pecans? Top the sweet potato mixture with coarsely chopped pecans just before putting on the marshmallows.

★★★

Star of the show!

★★★

Where to begin when meal planning…the main dish!

★★★

The Main Dish:

Bear Paw Quiche

We first enjoyed this quiche on the deck of a lovely bed and breakfast overlooking the Rocky Mountains in beautiful Winter Park, Colorado. We were delighted when the innkeepers, Sue and Rick, shared their recipe with us to make at home! Years later, we still enjoy this fabulous recipe for breakfast, lunch, or dinner!

Ingredients:

One 9"deep dish pie shell
2 tbsp. butter
½ small onion, chopped
1 c. fresh mushrooms, sliced
8 oz. cream cheese, cut into small cubes
1 c. fresh spinach, chopped
1 ½ c. grated Swiss cheese
1 ½ c. grated Monterey Jack cheese
6 large eggs
1 c. half-and-half

Instructions:

1. Preheat oven to 425 degrees.
2. In a large skillet over medium-high heat, melt butter and sauté onions; when they are tender, add mushrooms and cook until lightly browned.
3. Meanwhile, place the cubes of cream cheese onto the bottom of the pie shell.
4. Next add the cooked onions and mushrooms, spreading evenly over the pie shell; add the spinach, again, spreading evenly.
5. Sprinkle both grated cheeses over top of vegetables.
6. In a mixing bowl, beat together the milk and eggs; slowly pour mixture over the top of quiche.
7. Bake at 425 degrees for 15 minutes, and then reduce the oven temperature to 350 degrees and bake for another 30 minutes. Quiche should be golden. Enjoy!

Yield: 8 servings

Kitchen Kimberley's Tip:

❖ Serve this delicious quiche with fresh fruit, bacon or sausage for breakfast. For lunch or dinner, serve with a tossed green salad and crusty French bread.

Beef Tips with Gravy on Rice

Oh my goodness...the first time I made this recipe I fell 'head over heels' in love with it! The beef is so tender, and the gravy is thick, rich and delicious! When you need comfort food, this is the recipe for you!

Ingredients:

2 tbsp. shortening
2 lbs. beef tips
1 (10.75 oz.) can beef consommé
1/3 c. Burgundy wine
2 tbsp. soy sauce
¼ tsp. onion salt
¼ tsp. garlic salt
¼ tsp. seasoned salt
2 tbsp. cornstarch
¼ c. water
* Hot cooked rice

Instructions:

1. In a large Dutch oven, heat shortening over high heat. Brown beef tips on all sides, about 3 to 5 minutes.
2. Deglaze the pan by stirring in the beef consommé, wine, and soy sauce; bring to a boil, stirring and scraping up the bits from the bottom of the pan.
3. Add onion salt, garlic salt, and seasoned salt and reduce heat to low.
4. Cover and simmer for 1 hour or until meat is tender.
5. In a small bowl, blend cornstarch and water; stir gradually into meat mixture.
6. Cook and stir until mixture thickens, about 2 minutes.
7. Serve over hot cooked rice. Enjoy!

Yield: 8 servings

Kitchen Kimberley's Tips:

❖ Beef tips are just that – tips of beef from the sirloin flap. In fact, you may find them labeled as 'sirloin tips' at your market. You can also use 'stew meat' cut into ½-inch cubes.

❖ For a variation, this is also delicious when served over cooked egg noodles.

Bubbly Baked Ziti

This dish takes me way back...to my college days! As a student living in an off-campus apartment, I enjoyed making meals for my girlfriends in my tiny kitchen. Bubbly Baked Ziti was always a hit, and the girls would often bring salads and bread for a complete freshman feast! Good food and good friends certainly are a match made in heaven! This recipe serves 8.

Ingredients:

1 lb. lean ground beef
1 white onion, chopped
1 green pepper, chopped
1 medium zucchini, chopped
1 (14.5 oz.) can diced tomatoes in sauce
1 (8 oz.) can tomato sauce
1 ½ tsp. dried leaf basil
1 ½ tsp. dried leaf oregano
½ tsp. dried leaf parsley
½ tsp. garlic salt
½ tsp. freshly ground black pepper
½ lb. ziti or other shaped pasta, cooked and drained
8 oz. shredded mozzarella cheese

Instructions:

1. Preheat oven to 350 degrees.
2. In a large skillet over medium-high heat, cook and crumble beef with onions and peppers until meat is lightly browned; add zucchini and cook 5 minutes longer.
3. Add tomatoes, tomato sauce, basil, oregano, parsley, garlic salt and pepper; stir well.
4. Add ziti and half of the shredded cheese; stir well.
5. Transfer mixture to a lightly greased 9 x 13-inch baking dish, and sprinkle with remaining cheese. Bake, covered, for 20 to 25 minutes, or until hot and bubbly.
6. Uncover and bake 5 to 10 minutes longer, or until cheese is lightly browned. Enjoy!

Kitchen Kimberley's Tip:

❖ Try this recipe using Sweet Italian Sausage instead of ground beef for a flavorful variation!

California Chicken Enchiladas

My family first enjoyed this recipe when I was just 15 years old! I loved to help my Mom make these enchiladas, and we all loved eating them! Although these are not 'traditional' enchiladas, their rich onion flavor makes them very special!

Ingredients:

1 (15 oz.) can tomato sauce
1 clove garlic, finely chopped
1 ½ tsp. hot pepper sauce, *divided use*
1 c. sour cream
½ pkg. dry onion soup mix
2 c. Monterey Jack cheese, shredded, *divided use*
1 ½ c. cooked chicken, diced
1 (4 oz.) can diced green chiles, drained
12 corn tortillas
1 large green pepper, finely chopped

Instructions:

1. Preheat oven to 375 degrees.
2. In a small saucepan, combine tomato sauce, garlic and only ½ teaspoon of the hot pepper sauce; simmer 15 minutes.
3. Meanwhile, in a small bowl, blend together the sour cream and dry onion soup mix; this mixture is called *California Onion Dip*.
4. In a large bowl, combine 1 cup of the shredded cheese, the diced chicken, *California Onion Dip*, green chiles, and remaining hot sauce.
5. Place about 2 ½ tablespoons of this mixture down the center of each tortilla; roll up and place seam-side down in a greased 2-quart oblong baking dish.
6. Spoon the prepared sauce over enchiladas evenly, and then cover with remaining shredded cheese and sprinkle with chopped green pepper.
7. Bake, uncovered, for 15 to 20 minutes or until hot and bubbly, and cheese is melted. Enjoy!

Yield: 4 to 6 servings

Kitchen Kimberley's Tip:

❖ We prepared this recipe quite frequently when I was growing up. To keep it interesting, we would alternate between using corn tortillas and flour tortillas. Try it with both and see which one you prefer!

Cheddar Crunch Chicken

My kitchen is a 'no- fry zone', which means that I refuse to fry anything! So when it comes to chicken tenders, I played with a lot of ways to give the coating a nice crunchy texture packed with flavor. The results speak for themselves!   We love this 'un-fried' chicken, and hope you will, too!

Ingredients:

1/2 c. butter
4 cloves garlic, minced
1/2 c. plain dry bread crumbs
1/2 c. Ritz crackers, crushed (start with 15 crackers)
1/2 c. freshly grated Parmesan cheese
1 1/2 c. shredded Sharp Cheddar cheese
1 tsp. dried parsley
1/2 tsp. dried leaf oregano
1/4 tsp. ground black pepper
1 lb. chicken tenders

Instructions:

1. Preheat oven to 350 degrees.
2. In a small saucepan over low heat, melt the butter. Add garlic and cook until tender, about 3 minutes; remove from heat and allow to cool slightly.
3. Meanwhile, in a shallow bowl or pie plate, mix remaining ingredients, except chicken. Sprinkle 1/8 cup of the crumb mixture over the bottom of a 9 x 13-inch baking dish.
4. Dip each chicken tender into the garlic butter to coat well, and then press into the breading mixture, turning to coat well. Arrange coated chicken evenly in the baking dish. Drizzle with any remaining butter and top with remaining breadcrumb mixture. Bake for 20 minutes in preheated oven, or until chicken is no longer pink, and juices run clear. Enjoy!

Yield: 4 servings

Kitchen Kimberley's Tip:

❖ Buttermilk does wonders for chicken! Soak chicken in buttermilk for at least 4 hours to tenderize and add amazing flavor; drain, pat dry and proceed with recipe. It might sound silly, but buttermilk makes chicken taste more like...chicken!

Chicken Lickin' Pork Chops

This old-fashioned recipe has been a family favorite for decades, and we especially enjoy it in the fall. When I think of this recipe, I realize how food touches all the senses. Just now, I can hear the sizzle of the pork as it competes with the cheering and excitement of the football game on television. I can feel the cool breeze coming in through the open window that lets out all of the delicious aromas; I can almost see them as they waft into the crisp fall air. Then, I hear the doorbell...it's a neighbor coming over to see what smells so good! Yep – guess who's coming to dinner now?! You might want to double this recipe!

Ingredients:

4 medium pork chops (bone-in or boneless loin chops)
¼ c. butter-flavored shortening
¼ c. all-purpose flour
2 tsp. garlic salt
1 tsp. ground mustard
1 (10 ¾ oz.) can condensed chicken with rice soup
½ soup can of water
Optional: 4 cups cooked rice

Instructions:

1. Place flour, garlic salt and ground mustard in a pie plate (or other shallow dish) and blend well.
2. Dredge pork chops, coating very well.
3. In a heavy frying pan, melt shortening over medium-high heat; brown chops on both sides.
4. Add the soup and water to the pan, pouring the liquid around the chops, but not on top of them.
5. Reduce heat to low, cover and cook for 45 minutes or until tender.
6. Serve over a bed of rice, and enjoy!

Yield: 4 servings

Kitchen Kimberley's Tips:

- ❖ Boost the flavor of your rice by using chicken broth instead of plain water. Also, add a pop of color by stirring in a handful of chopped fresh parsley or chives to cooked rice.
- ❖ For a variation, try using bone-in, skin-on chicken breasts or thighs instead of pork...yum!

Chicken Spaghetti

My Mother-in-Law made this dish for us just after my husband and I started dating. It was so good that I had to make it for my own family, too! One taste of this scrumptious casserole and my parents knew I had found a 'keeper', in both the recipe and in my sweet Terry! Not only is it a blessing to have a wonderful mother-in-law, but mine is also a great cook!

Ingredients:

3 c. cooked, cubed chicken
1 tsp. olive oil
1 large yellow onion, chopped
14 oz. spaghetti
1 lb. processed cheese, diced
1 (10 ¾ oz.) can cream of chicken soup
1 (10 ¾ oz.) can cream of mushroom soup
1 (10 oz.) can diced tomatoes with green chiles
1 c. grated cheddar cheese, or more to taste

Instructions:

1. Preheat oven to 350 degrees.
2. In a large stock pot, heat the olive oil over medium-high heat and cook onions until tender, about 5 to 10 minutes, stirring occasionally.
3. Meanwhile, cook and drain spaghetti and add it to the cooked onion in the stock pot.
4. Stir in the diced processed cheese (while everything is still hot!) and the cream soups and tomatoes; blend well together.
5. Gently stir in the cooked chicken and spoon the mixture into a greased 9 x 13-inch baking dish.
6. Top with grated cheddar cheese and bake, uncovered, for about 30 minutes, or until casserole is hot and bubbly and cheese is melted.
7. Garnish with freshly snipped parsley or thinly sliced green onions. Enjoy!

Yield: 12 servings

Kitchen Kimberley's Tip:

❖ This comforting casserole is great to take to a friend or neighbor in need. You can easily divide this recipe into two smaller casserole dishes – just keep one and share one. Or, enjoy one now and freeze one for later!

Country Beans and Ham

A big pot of brown beans simmering away conjures up great memories for me! While growing up, beans were one of my favorite dinners, and I still love them today. Nothing comforts the soul quite like a big, steaming bowl of brown beans -- especially when they are topped with grated cheddar cheese and diced onions...and served with freshly baked corn bread so warm the butter slides right off! Serves 12

Ingredients:

1 lb. dry pinto beans
8 c. water
1 yellow onion, chopped
1 or 2 ham hocks
2 tbsp. garlic powder
2 tbsp. dry barbecue seasoning (use your favorite brand)
¼ tsp. freshly ground black pepper
2 c. cooked ham, coarsely chopped
Garnish: Chopped onions, shredded cheddar cheese, salsa, pickled jalapenos

Prep Ahead: Sort beans to remove any debris, rocks or discolored beans; rinse and drain well in a colander. Either soak in water overnight in the refrigerator, or simply use the 'quick-soak' method as I do: Boil beans in a large pot for 2 minutes; remove from heat; cover and let set for 1 hour. Both methods work equally as well. Whichever method you choose, be sure to drain and rinse the beans well.

Instructions:

1. Add beans to a large stockpot and cover with 8 cups of cold water.
2. Add chopped onion, ham hock (use 2 for more flavor) and seasonings; bring to a boil, reduce heat and slowly simmer for at least 2 hours, and preferably up to 6 hours, being careful to watch the water level, adding more water if necessary.
3. Thirty minutes prior to serving, remove the ham hock and discard. Add the 2 cups of chopped ham and continue to simmer for 30 minutes.
4. Serve beans piping hot with the optional toppings, if you like. Enjoy!

Kitchen Kimberley's Tip:

❖ Salt the beans to taste just prior to serving. Most barbecue seasoning blends include a good amount of salt, so the additional salt may not be necessary. Let your taste buds be the judge of that!

Cranberry Chicken

The gorgeous glaze on this chicken makes it pretty enough to serve for company, and oh, so flavorful! The ease of preparation means you can enjoy this as a weekday family meal, too! Cranberry and chicken were meant for each other!

Ingredients:

1 broiler-fryer chicken (3 to 4 pounds), cut up
½ tsp. salt
¼ tsp. freshly ground black pepper
2 tbsp. butter
½ c. chopped onion
½ c. chopped celery
1 (16 oz.) can whole-berry cranberry sauce
1 c. (your favorite) barbecue sauce

Instructions:

1. Preheat oven to 350 degrees.
2. Sprinkle chicken pieces with salt and pepper. In a large skillet, melt butter over medium-high heat.
3. Working in batches, brown chicken on all sides; transfer browned pieces to a greased 9 x 13 x 2-inch baking dish.
4. In same skillet, sauté onion and celery in the remaining drippings until tender.
5. Add cranberry and barbecue sauces; stir to mix well; pour over chicken.
6. Bake, uncovered for 1 ½ hours, or until juices run clear, basting every 15 minutes. Enjoy!

Yield: 4 to 6 servings

Kitchen Kimberley's Tip:

❖ Prefer all white meat? Use 3 to 4 pounds of bone-in chicken breasts.

Crock Pot Enchilada Casserole

Got a hungry crowd to feed? Then this recipe is just for you! Serve this delicious casserole alongside bowls of guacamole, salsa and sour cream, and let the feasting begin!

Ingredients:

2 ½ lbs. ground beef
1 large white onion, diced
3 tsp. chili powder
1 tsp. ground cumin
1 tsp. dried leaf oregano
1 pkg. taco seasoning mix
1 (10 ¾ oz.) can cream of mushroom soup
1 (10 ¾ oz.) can cream of chicken soup
½ c. beef broth
1 (4 oz.) can diced green chiles
1 (16 oz.) can red kidney, pinto or black beans, rinsed and drained
24 yellow corn tortillas, chopped into bite-sized pieces
1 ½ c. shredded cheddar cheese
1 ½ c. shredded Pepper Jack cheese

Instructions:

1. In a large skillet over medium-high heat, brown ground beef; drain well.
2. Add onion and seasonings to pan; cook until onion is tender.
3. Transfer beef mixture to a large bowl; add soups, broth, chiles and beans, mixing well.
4. In a 5-quart crock pot, layer 1/3 of the beef mixture with 1/3 of the corn tortillas and 1/3 of the cheeses; repeat layering twice.
5. Cover and cook on low heat for 5 hours. Enjoy!

Yield: 12 to 14 servings

Kitchen Kimberley's Tip:

❖ A simple green salad of shredded iceberg lettuce, red onion and tomatoes is the perfect complement to this comforting casserole. Make a southwest salad dressing by combining equal parts of your favorite salsa with Ranch dressing for a zippy flavor that will have your taste buds saying 'ole'!

Crock Pot French Dip Sandwiches

Full of rich, robust flavor, this recipe is sure to please a crowd! It is perfect for casual weekend entertaining or for busy weeknights when the family is eating on the run. What a treat to come home to a crock pot full of beefy goodness that everyone will love!

Ingredients:

4 lb. chuck roast, well-trimmed of fat
6 cloves garlic
1 (10.5 oz.) can beef broth
1 (10.5 oz.) can condensed French Onion soup
1 (12 oz.) can Coca-Cola Classic (not diet)
6 French rolls, or soft deli-style rolls
2 tbsp. butter

Instructions:

1. Using a sharp paring knife, cut 6 slits into the roast; place a garlic clove into each cut, deep into the meat. Place roast into crock-pot.
2. Add the beef broth, condensed French onion soup, and cola.
3. Cover and cook on low setting for 6 to 8 hours or on high for 4 hours.
4. Carefully remove beef from crock pot (it will be very tender!); cover with foil to keep warm.
5. Preheat oven to 350 degrees. Spread rolls with butter and toast in preheated oven for about 10 minutes, or until lightly toasted.
6. Slice or shred the meat and serve on toasted rolls. Serve with the warm sauce for dipping. Enjoy!

Yield: 6 servings

Kitchen Kimberley's Tip:

❖ For a variation, I like to make *'French Dip Sliders'* by serving these on individual hot rolls. You can find these either in the bread aisle or in the bakery at your local grocery store. Make these sandwiches even better by adding a slice of provolone or Swiss cheese!

Easy Oven Omelette

For years my family enjoyed this as the main attraction of our Christmas Morning Brunch. My Mom loved to make this for us (adult) kids, and of course, Dad helped her break the 18 eggs! Get a helper if you can, this takes a little time but it is worth every minute!   This is a great dish to make ahead for overnight guests!

Ingredients:

2 tsp. butter
18 large eggs
1 c. sour cream
1 c. milk
2 tsp. salt
¼ tsp. dried leaf basil
2 c. shredded cheddar cheese
1 (4 oz.) can mushrooms, drained
4 green onions, with tops, thinly sliced
1 (2 oz.) jar diced pimiento, drained

Instructions:

1. Preheat oven to 325 degrees.
2. In preheated oven, melt butter in a 9 x 13 x 2-inch baking dish, tilt dish to coat bottom with butter.
3. In a large mixing bowl, beat eggs, sour cream, milk, salt and basil until blended. Stir in cheese, mushrooms, green onions and pimiento; pour mixture into buttered baking dish.
4. Bake, uncovered, until omelette is set but still moist, about 45 minutes.
5. Allow omelette to set for about 5 minutes, and then cut into 12 (3-inch) squares. Garnish with additional sliced green onion tops, if desired. Enjoy!

Yield: 12 to 14 servings

Kitchen Kimberley's Tips:

- ❖ To make this ahead, after pouring mixture into baking dish, cover and refrigerate no longer than 24 hours. Bake omelette, uncovered in 325-degree oven for 50 to 55 minutes. Remember – a cold dish always goes into a cold oven to warm gently; put the cold dish in, then heat the oven.

- ❖ Serve this like my Mom did with fresh fruit, coffee cake or cinnamon rolls, bacon or sausage and lots of love!

Honey Nut Salmon

We love to cruise Alaska, and we especially enjoy the abundance of fresh salmon there. This recipe was inspired when we attended an outdoor salmon bake in Juneau, the capital. The simple marriage of tangy and sweet sauce paired with the contrast of tender, flaky salmon and crunchy pecans is a delight for salmon lovers!

Ingredients:

4 (4 oz.) salmon fillets, skin removed
¾ c. honey
¼ c. soy sauce
1 tbsp. balsamic vinegar
4 cloves garlic, minced
2 tbsp. butter
1 c. finely chopped pecans

Instructions:

1. In a small saucepan over low heat, combine the honey, soy sauce, balsamic vinegar, garlic and butter, until blended and smooth; remove from heat and allow mixture to cool slightly.
2. Meanwhile, place salmon fillets in a shallow dish; pour cooled mixture over fillets and turn once to coat both sides of fish evenly.
3. Cover and marinate in refrigerator for 2 hours, turning once.
4. When ready to cook, preheat oven to 350 degrees.
5. Remove salmon from marinade and transfer to a foil-lined shallow baking sheet.
6. Press chopped pecans firmly onto the top of each salmon fillet. Bake for 20 to 25 minutes or until salmon flakes easily with a fork. Enjoy!

Yield: 4 servings

Kitchen Kimberley's Tips:

- ❖ No pecans on hand? No problem! Try this recipe with chopped macadamia nuts, walnuts, almonds or cashews for a nutty variation.

- ❖ Serve this salmon on a bed of cooked wild rice, with roasted asparagus spears on the side for an easy and elegant meal.

Hoppin' John

The city of Charleston, South Carolina is packed with history as well as fabulous restaurants! On a recent trip there, I enjoyed this dish in a quaint downtown restaurant on Market Street. As soon as I returned home I started trying to re-create the flavors I had enjoyed in that authentic Southern dish, and the resulting recipe is this flavorful Midwest version that we now enjoy frequently. Serves 8.

Ingredients:

1 tsp. olive oil
1 smoked sausage link, diced
1 c. uncooked brown or white rice
1 medium onion, chopped
1 medium red bell pepper, chopped
½ medium green bell pepper, chopped
3 ribs celery, chopped
1 large clove garlic, minced
2 c. water
1 (10 oz.) can diced tomatoes with green chiles
2 (15 oz.) cans black eyed peas, rinsed and drained
1 tsp. Old Bay seasoning
½ tsp. dried thyme leaves
¾ tsp. ground cumin
1 bay leaf
4 green onions, thinly sliced (stir in just before serving)

Instructions:

1. In a large, heavy pan heat oil over medium-high heat. Add diced smoked sausage and rice; sauté for 2 minutes. Add onions, peppers, and celery; sauté 5 minutes or until softened. Stir in garlic; cook, stirring constantly for 1 minute.
2. Add all remaining ingredients except green onions; bring to a boil, cover and cook for 20 minutes or until rice has absorbed the water.
3. Remove bay leaf; stir in the sliced green onions and serve. Enjoy!

Kitchen Kimberley's Tip:

❖ Use your family's favorite – either brown or white rice for this recipe; simply adjust the cooking time according to the directions on the rice package.

Nacho Chicken

When the temperatures are dipping, this hot casserole will surely warm you up! Serve this with my Mom's Spanish Rice, and my Easy Charro Beans for a complete Mexican fiesta for your taste buds!

Ingredients:

4 c. cooked chicken, cut into bite-sized pieces
1 (16 oz.) pkg. processed cheese, cubed
2 (10 ¾ oz.) cans cream of chicken soup
1 (10 oz.) can diced tomatoes with green chiles
1 (4 oz.) can diced green chiles
1 c. minced onion
½ tsp. garlic salt
¼ tsp. freshly ground black pepper
1 (11.5 oz.) bag nacho cheese tortilla chips, lightly crushed
1 c. shredded cheddar cheese

Instructions:

1. Preheat oven to 350 degrees.
2. In a large bowl, combine chicken, cheese, cream of chicken soup, tomatoes, green chiles, onion, and seasonings. Stir in crushed tortilla chips.
3. Spoon mixture into a greased 9 x 13 x 2-inch baking dish; sprinkle with shredded cheddar cheese. Bake, uncovered, for 20 minutes; uncover and bake 10 minutes longer or until cheese is melted and casserole is hot and bubbly. Enjoy!

Yield: 8 to 10 servings

Kitchen Kimberley's Tips:

❖ Garnish with thinly sliced green onions, or freshly snipped cilantro.

❖ For milder flavor, substitute one can of plain diced tomatoes for the diced tomatoes with green chiles.

Orange Glazed Cornish Hens

These gorgeous glazed hens are an easy, yet elegant entrée to serve for a cozy dinner party of four.

Ingredients:

4 Cornish game hens (22 ounces each)
¼ c. unsalted butter, melted
1 tsp. salt
½ tsp. freshly ground black pepper
¾ c. fresh orange juice
½ c. packed light brown sugar
½ c. chicken broth
2 tbsp. fresh lemon juice
1 tsp. ground mustard
¼ tsp. ground allspice

Instructions:

1. Preheat oven to 350 degrees.
2. Rinse hens and pat dry.
3. Tie the legs of each hen together; turn wing tips under backs.
4. Place on a greased rack in a roasting pan; brush hens with melted butter, then sprinkle with salt and pepper.
5. Bake, uncovered, for 1 hour.
6. Meanwhile, in a small saucepan, bring remaining ingredients to a boil over medium-high heat. Reduce heat; simmer, uncovered for 15 minutes.
7. Spoon sauce mixture over hens. Bake 15 minutes longer, or until a meat thermometer reads 180 degrees F. Enjoy!

Yield: 4 servings

Kitchen Kimberley's Tip:

❖ Serve these hens with wild rice pilaf and my *Pear Salad with Sugared Walnuts (page 57)*. Add a loaf of crusty bread and you have an easy menu for entertaining!

Perfect Pot Roast

Long ago I believed that the crock-pot was the only way to successfully cook a tender roast, but that all changed once I cooked up this recipe! Browning the meat and then slow roasting it in the oven makes it so tender you can cut it with a fork! Best of all, this recipe creates its own delicious beef gravy, as well!

Ingredients:

½ c. all-purpose flour
1 tsp. garlic powder
1 tsp. onion powder
1 tsp. paprika
½ tsp. seasoned salt
½ tsp. freshly ground black pepper
3 ½ lbs. rump roast
¼ c. butter
1 (10 ¾ oz.) can cream of mushroom soup
1 (10.75 oz.) can beef consommé
2 tbsp. dried onion flakes
1 tbsp. salt-free all-purpose seasoning
1 tsp. onion powder

Instructions:

1. Preheat oven to 325 degrees.
2. In a large mixing bowl, combine the flour, garlic powder, onion powder, paprika, seasoned salt and pepper; dredge the roast in the seasoned flour to coat evenly. Shake off excess coating.
3. In a large Dutch oven over medium-high heat, melt the butter and brown the roast on all sides.
4. Deglaze the pan by adding half of the beef consommé, scraping the bottom of the pan to loosen browned bits.
5. In a small bowl, combine cream of mushroom soup and all remaining ingredients, blending well. Pour mixture over roast.
6. Cover and bake for 3 hours; remove from oven and allow meat to rest for 15 minutes before slicing and serving. Enjoy!

Yield: 8 servings

Kitchen Kimberley's Tip:

❖ During the last hour of cooking, add carrots and potatoes, if desired.

Roasted Turkey Breast with Herbed Butter

The buttery herb mixture melts slowly into the meat as this turkey roasts to a perfectly golden brown in the oven. Having so many flavors and being so much easier than roasting a whole turkey...this is a recipe for which to be thankful!

Ingredients:

½ c. unsalted butter, softened
1 tsp. fresh lemon juice
½ c. fresh parsley, chopped
¼ c. freshly snipped chives
½ tsp. dried leaf basil
½ tsp. dried leaf marjoram
1 (7 to 8-lb.) bone-in turkey breast
1 yellow onion, quartered
1 bay leaf
¼ c. olive oil
Salt and freshly ground black pepper

Instructions:

1. Prepare herbed butter by combining first 6 ingredients either by hand, or in a small food processor; set aside.
2. Preheat oven to 325 degrees.
3. Rinse turkey breast well; pat dry with paper towel. Using your hands or a small rubber spatula, loosen skin from breast meat. Spread some of the herbed butter between skin and meat; season turkey inside and out with salt and pepper.
4. Place the onion and bay leaf inside the turkey. Rub olive oil and remaining herbed butter over the turkey skin.
5. Place turkey on a v-rack in a shallow roasting pan. Cover securely with a foil tent, and roast until a meat thermometer registers 170 degrees when inserted into the thickest part of the breast, not touching the bone; this should take between 2 ¼ to 3¼ hours.
6. Remove from oven and allow turkey to rest, covered, for at least 20 minutes. Remove seasonings from cavity; garnish, carve and enjoy!

Kitchen Kimberley's Tip:

❖ For even more flavor, roast this turkey on a bed of thick-sliced onions, carrots and potatoes instead of a v-rack. The vegetables impart wonderful flavor as the meat roasts. Yield: 8 servings

Smothered Chicken and Vegetables

By far, this is one of my most popular recipes of all time, and it could not be easier to prepare! My husband requests this one frequently, so to keep it interesting I serve it over biscuits one time, and over rice the next. It is also delicious served over egg noodles! With this recipe, no matter how it is served, you cannot go wrong!

Ingredients:

1 tbsp. olive oil
¾ lb. boneless, skinless chicken breast, diced
1 (10 ¾ oz.) can condensed cream of mushroom soup
½ c. sour cream
1 tbsp. dried minced onion
1 tbsp. crushed red pepper flakes
1 tsp. garlic powder
2 c. frozen mixed vegetables (your choice), thawed
* Hot biscuits, cooked rice or pasta of your choice

Instructions:

1. Heat olive oil in a large skillet over medium-high heat.
2. Cook the diced chicken, stirring frequently, until no longer pink.
3. Add all remaining ingredients and stir to combine well; simmer for 20 minutes.
4. Serve over the hot biscuits, cooked rice, or pasta of your choice. Enjoy!

Yield: 4 servings

Kitchen Kimberley's Tips:

❖ For an easy variation, try using a different flavor of cream soup. My suggestions include, cream of chicken, cream of mushroom with roasted garlic, or broccoli cheese.

❖ Make this recipe lighter on the waistline by using one of the reduced fat cream soups, and/or reduced fat sour cream.

Stromboli

Allow me to introduce you to one of my favorite childhood dinners! It will be a delight when your taste buds meet this crusty bread filled with perfectly- seasoned beefy sauce topped with gooey-melted Mozzarella cheese! Enough said – let's eat Stromboli! Depending on how much you love this recipe, it serves around 6 people.

Ingredients:

1 lb. ground beef
1 c. chopped onion
1 c. chopped green pepper
1 (12 oz.) can tomato paste
½ c. quick cooking oats, uncooked
½ cup water
1 (2 ½ oz.) can mushrooms, drained
1 tsp. salt
1 tsp. Italian seasoning
¼ tsp. garlic powder
1 (1 lb.) Vienna bread loaf
12 oz. Mozzarella cheese, thinly sliced

Instructions:

1. Preheat oven to 400 degrees.
2. In a large skillet, brown ground beef with onions and green peppers, until beef is no longer pink.
3. Stir in tomato paste, oats, water, mushrooms and seasonings. Stir to blend well; simmer, uncovered for about 10 minutes.
4. Meanwhile, slice Vienna bread loaf lengthwise using a serrated knife. Hollow out bread, leaving a ½ -inch shell on bottoms and sides of both halves.
5. Please half of the cheese slices on the bottom half; spoon the warm meat mixture on top of the cheese. Lay remaining cheese slices on meat, then top with other half of bread.
6. Wrap tightly in foil and place onto a large baking sheet. Bake for 15 to 18 minutes, or until bread is crispy on the outside. Enjoy!

Kitchen Kimberley's Tip:

❖ Prefer fresh mushrooms? Substitute ½ cup of chopped fresh ones for the canned; use your favorite variety.

"Too Easy" Chicken Pot Pie

When you need a speedy and simple dish that the whole family will enjoy, try this one! With comforting flavors, creamy texture, chunks of tender chicken and a flaky crust on top, this is sure to become a new family favorite! Best of all – it comes together so quickly that you will have dinner on the table in record time! While it's baking, throw together a green salad and you've got a complete meal to enjoy.

Ingredients:

2 c. diced cooked chicken breasts
1 (10 ¾ oz.) can condensed cream of chicken soup
1 (10 ¾ oz.) can condensed cream of potato soup
½ tsp. garlic powder
¼ tsp. freshly ground black pepper
Dash of poultry seasoning
2 c. frozen mixed vegetables, rinsed to thaw, and drained
1 box (15 oz.) refrigerated pie crust, softened as directed on box
Egg wash: One egg yolk with ½ tsp. of water – mix well.

Instructions:

1. Preheat oven to 400 degrees.
2. In a large bowl combine the chicken, soups, seasonings and vegetables well.
3. Line a 9-inch pie plate with one crust, and pour in the filling mixture.
4. Top with the other pie crust, tucking top crust behind the bottom crust around the edges; crimp as desired to seal edges well.
5. Brush with egg wash, and cut two small slits in the top crust to vent.
6. Bake, uncovered, for 20 to 30 minutes, or until crust is golden brown. If edges of crust begin to brown too quickly, simply cover them with foil.

Yield: 6 servings

Kitchen Kimberley's Tip:

❖ Use your favorite frozen mixed vegetable blend for this recipe. We prefer to keep it simple with just a blend of peas and carrots, but any mixed vegetables would be delicious!

Turkey Stuffing Casserole

All of the best flavors of Thanksgiving are found in every yummy bite of this casserole! It is a wonderful way to enjoy some of your leftover holiday turkey, and a quick and easy main course that the whole family will love!

Ingredients:

2 c. cooked, cubed turkey
3 c. soft white bread, crust removed, cubed
6 tbsp. melted butter
2 tbsp. finely chopped onion
2 tbsp. finely chopped celery
1 tsp. poultry seasoning
½ tsp. salt
¼ tsp. freshly ground black pepper
1 packet turkey gravy mix, or 1 cup prepared turkey gravy

Instructions:

1. Preheat oven to 350 degrees.
2. In a large mixing bowl, combine turkey, bread cubes, butter, onion, and seasonings; toss lightly.
3. Arrange mixture evenly in a greased 1-quart casserole dish; press lightly.
4. If using gravy mix, prepare according to package directions. Pour prepared gravy over top of casserole.
5. Bake for 35 to 40 minutes. Enjoy!

Yield: 6 servings

Kitchen Kimberley's Tips:

❖ Enjoy this recipe year-round by substituting cooked chicken for the turkey, and chicken gravy for the turkey gravy.

❖ Serve this recipe with my Cashew and Apple Salad, Southern Green Beans, and hot rolls for a delicious dinner!

Upside-Down Ham Loaf

Leftover holiday ham never tasted so good!   This recipe is one of my favorite childhood dishes, and my family still loves it.

Ingredients:

1 tbsp. butter
1 tbsp. brown sugar
1 (8 oz.) can crushed pineapple, drained, juice reserved
3 c. cooked ground ham
Reserved juice (should be ¼ cup) from pineapple
¼ c. grated onion
¼ tsp. dry mustard
¾ c. plain dry bread crumbs
2 eggs, slightly beaten
Dash cayenne pepper
4 oz. Swiss cheese, shredded

Instructions:

1. Preheat oven to 350 degrees.
2. Melt butter in the bottom of a greased 8 ½ x 4 ½ x 2 ½ -inch loaf pan; sprinkle brown sugar over melted butter.
3. Spoon the drained crushed pineapple over brown sugar.
4. In a large mixing bowl, combine ground ham with all remaining ingredients except cheese; pack half of this mixture over the pineapple, then sprinkle cheese on top.
5. Pack remaining ham mixture over cheese.
6. Bake, covered, for 45 to 50 minutes. Let stand 5 minutes before carefully inverting onto a platter for serving. Enjoy!

Yield: 8 servings

Kitchen Kimberley's Tip:

❖ Our family of four always had leftovers, so the next day my Mom would thinly slice it for 'ham loaf sandwiches' to serve at lunchtime. As a sandwich, the pineapple, ham and Swiss cheese tasted fabulous when served on whole-grain bread spread with a little Dijon mustard. Yum!

★★★

Breads

From Quick Bread to Cornbread…

and everything in between!

★★★

Breads:

Butter Pecan Bread

Quick breads are fabulous to bake in fall and winter. They are simple and versatile! For breakfast serve them plain or toasted, with cream cheese or jam. For dessert try topping a thick slice with your favorite ice cream and a drizzle of dessert sauce!

Ingredients:

2 ¼ c. all-purpose flour
2 tbsp. baking powder
½ tsp. baking soda
½ tsp. salt
½ tsp. cinnamon
¼ tsp. nutmeg
1 c. packed light brown sugar
1 c. chopped pecans
1 egg, slightly beaten
1 c. buttermilk
2 tbsp. unsalted butter, melted

Instructions:

1. Preheat oven to 350 degrees.
2. In a large bowl sift together the dry ingredients, then stir in pecans.
3. Combine remaining ingredients in a separate bowl, and then add to dry mixture; stir just until softened.
4. Transfer batter to a greased 9 x 5-inch loaf pan.
5. Bake for 45 minutes or until a toothpick inserted in the center comes out clean.
6. Cool slightly before removing from pan to cool on a wire rack.

Yield: 1 loaf

Kitchen Kimberley's Tips:

❖ While any bread is scrumptious when slathered with softened butter, it is easy to make an even more decadent flavored butter.

❖ To make *Maple Pecan Butter*, beat together one stick of softened butter with ½ cup of powdered sugar and ¼ cup of maple syrup; stir in ¼ cup of chopped pecans. Enjoy!

Cheddar Bundt Bread

Delight everyone by serving this savory and elegant loaf on a footed cake stand!

Filling Ingredients:

½ c. unsalted butter, at room temperature
¼ tsp. dried marjoram
¼ tsp. dried thyme
2 tbsp. finely minced onion
1 tbsp. finely minced parsley
1 c. grated extra-sharp cheddar cheese

Bread Ingredients:

2 ½ c. all-purpose flour
2 tbsp. granulated sugar
1 tsp. salt
2 pkgs. active dry yeast
½ c. milk
½ c. water
¼ c. butter, at room temperature
1 large egg, slightly beaten

Instructions:

1. In a small bowl, combine the butter, marjoram, thyme, onion and parsley; mix well. Stir in the cheese, and set aside.
2. In a large mixing bowl, combine 1 ½ cups of the flour with the sugar, salt, and yeast; mix well and set aside.
3. In a small saucepan, combine the milk, water, and butter; heat over medium-low heat until butter is melted and the milk is warm.
4. Add the milk mixture to the flour mixture along with the beaten egg.
5. Blend at low speed until moistened, and then beat at medium speed for 3 minutes. By hand, gradually add the remaining flour to make a stiff batter.
6. Generously grease a 9 or 10-inch tube pan or Bundt pan.
7. Spoon half of the batter into the pan, spreading evenly. Spread the filling over the dough, top with the remaining batter, and pat it on firmly.
8. Cover with a slightly dampened cloth and place in a warm area to rise until doubled in size (about 1 hour).
9. Meanwhile, preheat oven to 375. Bake bread for 35 to 40 minutes, or until golden brown. Remove from oven and immediately tip the bread out onto a wire rack to cool slightly before serving warm with butter. Enjoy!

Chocolate Chip Zucchini Bread

Whether served at breakfast or as an after-school snack, this sweet bread is sure to be a hit with everyone, including the kids! My Mom always had a fresh loaf made and one in the freezer, as well. But when my sister Sabrina came home for a visit, Mom always had two fresh loaves waiting for her -- one to enjoy during her visit, and one for her to take back home to Texas!

Ingredients:

3 eggs
2 c. granulated sugar
1 c. vegetable oil
1 tsp. salt
3 c. all-purpose flour
3 tsp. ground cinnamon
¼ tsp. baking powder
1 tsp. baking soda
2 c. grated zucchini
3 tsp. vanilla extract
1 ½ c. chopped pecans or walnuts
6 oz. semi-sweet mini chocolate chips

Instructions:

1. Preheat oven to 325 degrees.
2. Butter and flour two 8 ½ x 4 ½ x 2 ½ -inch loaf pans. (Note: 9 x 5-inch pans work fine, too.)
3. Beat the eggs in a large mixing bowl until foamy; stir in the sugar and oil, and blend thoroughly.
4. In a large bowl, sift together the salt, flour, cinnamon, baking powder and baking soda. Add this to the egg mixture, a third at a time, beating thoroughly after each addition; the mixture should be stiff.
5. Stir in the zucchini and vanilla. Fold in nuts and chocolate chips. When thoroughly blended, pour the mixture into the prepared pans.
6. Bake for 1 hour or until a knife inserted into the center comes out clean. Allow to cool in pans for 20 minutes, and then turn out onto a wire rack to cool completely.

Kitchen Kimberley's Tip:

❖ Since this makes 2 generous loaves, you can either freeze one, or share one with a neighbor or friend.

Cinnamon Carrot Bread

Carrots add both flavor and moist texture in this delicious bread! Parents, this is a great way to get your kids to eat some veggies! Serve this with breakfast, or as an after school snack.

Ingredients:

1 ½ c. all-purpose flour
1 tsp. ground cinnamon
½ tsp. baking soda
¼ tsp. salt
¼ tsp. baking powder
¼ tsp. ground nutmeg
½ c. granulated sugar
½ c. packed light brown sugar
1 c. grated carrots
½ c. canola oil
1 egg
½ c. chopped pecans
½ c. raisins

Instructions:

1. Preheat oven to 350 degrees.
2. In a large mixing bowl, combine the flour, cinnamon, baking soda, salt, baking powder, and nutmeg.
3. In another bowl, stir together the sugars, carrots, oil, and egg; add wet mixture to the dry ingredients, stirring just until dry ingredients are moistened.
4. Fold in nuts and raisins; spoon mixture into a greased 8 x 4 x 2-inch loaf pan.
5. Bake for 1 hour or until a toothpick inserted near the center comes out clean. Cool in pan for 10 minutes, and then remove to a wire rack to cool completely.
6. Wrap tightly in foil and store overnight before serving, for best flavor.

Yield: 1 loaf

Festive Fruit and Nut Bread

My husband is not a fan of eggnog, but he requests this delicious bread every year during the holidays! It is a treat with breakfast, or as an afternoon snack!

Bread Ingredients:

2 ½ c. all-purpose flour
2 tsp. baking powder
1 tsp. salt
¾ c. granulated sugar
½ c. coarsely chopped pecans
1 (8 oz.) pkg. diced candied mixed fruit
2 eggs, beaten
1 c. eggnog
¼ c. butter, melted

Glaze Ingredients:

1 c. powdered sugar
2 tbsp. eggnog

Instructions:

1. Preheat oven to 350 degrees.
2. Grease a 9 x 5-inch loaf pan; set aside.
3. In a large mixing bowl, sift together the flour, baking powder, salt and sugar. Add pecans and mixed fruit; stir until blended.
4. In a separate bowl, combine the eggs, eggnog and butter; add to dry ingredients, mixing only until dry ingredients are moistened.
5. Pour batter into prepared loaf pan; bake for 1 hour and 15 minutes; cool in pan for 1 hour, then remove to a wire rack to cool completely.
6. Prepare glaze by combining powdered sugar with eggnog until smooth. Spread glaze over cooled bread and garnish with additional candied fruit, if desired. Store in refrigerator. Enjoy!

Yield: 1 loaf

Gold Rush Cornbread

After the first bite of this tender and sweet cornbread melts in your mouth...you'll think you have struck gold with this recipe! By far, it is the best homemade cornbread I have ever tasted. I sure hope you enjoy it as much as we do!

Ingredients:

1 c. yellow cornmeal
1 c. milk
1 c. all-purpose flour
1/3 c. packed light brown sugar
1/3 c. granulated sugar
3 ½ tsp. baking powder
1 tsp. salt
1 egg
1/3 c. canola oil

Instructions:

1. Preheat oven to 400 degrees. Spray or lightly grease an 11 x 7-inch baking dish.
2. In a mixing bowl, combine the cornmeal and milk; soak together for 10 to 15 minutes.
3. In a separate bowl, combine the flour, brown sugar, sugar, baking powder and salt. Stir in the egg, canola oil and cornmeal-milk mixture until well combined. Pour batter into prepared pan.
4. Bake in preheated oven for 20 to 25 minutes, or until a toothpick inserted into the center of the pan comes out clean. Slather generously with real butter, and enjoy!

Yield: 12 servings

Kitchen Kimberley's Tips:

❖ This recipe can also be baked in a 9-inch round cake pan.

❖ Serve this delicious cornbread with my *Country Beans and Ham*, or any of the hearty soups or stews featured in this cookbook.

Lemon Cranberry Loaves

With a perfect blend of tart, tangy and sweet, these delicate loaves are a treat for everyone! Every year during the holidays I bake several batches of these loaves for friends and family to enjoy. They make great holiday gifts from the kitchen!

Ingredients:

1 ¼ c. finely chopped fresh cranberries
½ c. finely chopped walnuts
¼ c. granulated sugar
1 box lemon supreme cake mix
1 (3 oz.) pkg. cream cheese, softened
¾ c. milk
4 eggs
Powdered sugar, for garnish

Instructions:

1. Preheat oven to 350 degrees.
2. Grease and flour two 8 ½ x 4 ½ -inch loaf pans.
3. In a large bowl, stir together the cranberries, walnuts and sugar; set aside.
4. In another large bowl, combine cake mix, cream cheese and milk; beat at medium speed with electric mixer for 2 minutes. Add eggs, 1 at a time, beating for an additional 2 minutes.
5. Fold in cranberry mixture; pour batter into prepared loaf pans.
6. Bake for 45 to 50 minutes or until a toothpick inserted in the center comes out clean; cool in pans for 15 minutes.
7. Loosen loaves from pans and carefully invert onto a cooling rack. Turn loaves right side up to cool completely. Dust with powdered sugar. Enjoy!

Yield: 2 loaves

Kitchen Kimberley's Tips:

❖ Keep a bag of cranberries in the freezer for quick breads like this one.

❖ For an easy variation, make *'Spiced Cranberry Loaves'* by substituting a box of Spice Cake mix for the Lemon Supreme Cake mix.

Monkey Bread

When I asked my friends for suggestions on what to include in this cookbook, many of them said 'Monkey Bread'! It is easy to make and elegant to serve on a footed cake stand. Get the kids involved in the preparation and it will be ready in no time!

Ingredients:

2 c. chopped pecans, *divided use*
½ c. butter
1 c. packed light brown sugar
2 tbsp. water
2 cans flaky refrigerated biscuits

Instructions:

1. Preheat oven to 350 degrees.
2. Grease a tube pan or Bundt pan well; sprinkle 1 cup of the chopped pecans over bottom of pan.
3. In a small saucepan over medium heat, melt the butter and add sugar, water and remaining cup of pecans; stir to combine well.
4. Cut each biscuit in half and roll up, forming a total of 40 balls. Place 20 balls in the pan, and drizzle with half of the buttery mixture.
5. Place remaining 20 balls in pan and top with remaining mixture.
6. Bake for 20 to 25 minutes; allow bread to remain in pan for five minutes before inverting onto a pretty serving platter. Enjoy!

Yield: 8 servings

Kitchen Kimberley's Tips:

❖ The variations on this recipe are virtually endless! Add cinnamon to the glaze, or raisins in between the layers. This is a recipe you can really play with according to your own personal taste.

❖ Try adding a tiny cube of cream cheese inside each ball, or even a chunk of chocolate. Have fun in the kitchen, and enjoy the tasty results!

Orange Glazed Pecan Pie Muffins

When I was growing up, my Mom used to jokingly say that it was okay to eat a piece of Pecan Pie for breakfast because it had so many eggs in it! Well, we never actually ate pie for breakfast, but when we found this recipe the whole family decided that Pecan Pie Muffins were a great way to start our day!

Pecan Pie Muffin Ingredients:

1 c. firmly packed light brown sugar
½ c. all-purpose flour
1 c. chopped pecans
2/3 c. butter, melted
2 eggs

Orange Glaze Ingredients:

½ c. packed brown sugar
Grated zest of one fresh orange
Juice of one fresh orange

Instructions:

1. Preheat oven to 350 degrees.
2. In a large mixing bowl, combine the brown sugar, flour and pecans.
3. In a separate bowl, whisk together the butter and eggs; add to dry mixture, stirring just until moistened.
4. Fill muffin cups 2/3 full; bake for 20 to 25 minutes.
5. Meanwhile, heat the glaze ingredients in a small saucepan over low heat just until sugar is dissolved; remove from heat. Slowly spoon glaze over warm muffins. Enjoy!

Yield: 1 dozen muffins

Kitchen Kimberley's Tip:

❖ Refrigerate leftover muffins in an airtight container. Reheat or simply enjoy them cold!

Savory Cheddar and Chive Bread

Cheese lovers…this one is for you! Enjoy this loaf warm from the oven with a steaming bowl of your favorite soup, or slice and toast it up for savory sandwiches.

Ingredients:

2 c. all-purpose flour
4 tsp. baking powder
1 tbsp. granulated sugar
1 tsp. garlic powder
½ tsp. onion salt
½ tsp. dried leaf oregano
¼ tsp. ground mustard
¼ c. dried chives
1 ¼ c. shredded sharp cheddar cheese
1 egg, well beaten
1 c. milk
1 tbsp. butter, melted and cooled

Instructions:

1. Preheat oven to 350 degrees.
2. In a large mixing bowl, combine flour, baking powder, sugar, garlic powder, onion salt, oregano, ground mustard, chives and cheese; set aside.
3. In a small bowl, whisk together the egg, milk and melted butter.
4. Add wet ingredients all at once to dry ingredients, stirring just until moistened.
5. Spread batter into a greased 8 ½ x 4 ½ - inch loaf pan.
6. Bake for 45 minutes. If desired, brush the top of the loaf with additional melted butter as soon as it comes out of the oven.   Enjoy!

Yield: 1 loaf

Kitchen Kimberley's Tip:

❖ Try this bread for your next Grilled Cheese Sandwich! You will love it! My favorite Grilled Cheese includes finely chopped onion and green peppers, and crispy slices of bacon. Now that's how to eat a Grilled Cheese!

Southern Biscuits

A good biscuit recipe is something that no home cook should be without, so this one is for you! These tender biscuits are delicious when slathered with butter or fruit preserves, but they are also good for sopping up gravy!

Ingredients:

3 c. all-purpose flour
1 tbsp. baking powder
1 tbsp. granulated sugar
1 tsp. salt
¾ tsp. cream of tartar
½ c. unsalted butter
¼ c. shortening
1 c. milk

Instructions:

1. Preheat oven to 450 degrees.
2. In a large bowl, combine the flour, baking powder, granulated sugar, salt and cream of tartar.
3. Using a pastry blender, cut in the butter and shortening until mixture resembles coarse crumbs.
4. Make a well in the center of the flour mixture; add milk all at once. Using a fork, stir just until mixture is moistened.
5. Turn dough out onto a lightly floured surface. Knead dough by folding and gently pressing it for four to six strokes or just until dough holds together.
6. Pat or lightly roll dough until ¾ -inch thick. Cut dough with a floured 2 ½ - inch biscuit cutter; reroll scraps as necessary and dip cutter into flour between cuts.
7. Place dough circles 1 inch apart on an ungreased baking sheet. Bake for 10 to 14 minutes or until golden. Remove biscuits from baking sheet and serve warm. Enjoy!

Yield: 12 biscuits

Kitchen Kimberley's Tip:

❖ No time to roll in the dough? Make drop biscuits! Simply increase milk to 1 ¼ cups and follow recipe through step 4. Next, using a large spoon, drop the dough into 12 mounds on a *greased* baking sheet. Bake as directed above.

The Yummiest Banana Bread *Ever!*

Funny name, yes, but after just one taste of this moist, delicious banana bread, you will surely understand how it came to be known as the yummiest ever! This is not traditional banana bread, but it is definitely our family favorite!

Ingredients:

1 (18 oz.) box butter recipe yellow cake mix
4 bananas, mashed
3 eggs, slightly beaten
½ c. melted butter
½ c. chopped nuts
1 tsp. vanilla

Instructions:

1. Preheat oven to 350 degrees.
2. Coat 2 (9 x 5-inch) loaf pans with non-stick cooking spray.
3. In a large mixing bowl, blend all ingredients well.
4. Pour mixture evenly into the two prepared loaf pans.
5. Bake for 45 minutes to 1 hour, or until toothpick inserted into the center comes out clean. Enjoy!

Yield: 2 loaves

Kitchen Kimberley's Tips:

❖ For the best flavor, use very ripe bananas for baking bread. If the skins are dark and the bananas are very soft, then they are perfect for baking banana bread.

❖ This banana bread is delicious when toasted and spread with peanut butter. It also makes a scrumptious peanut butter and jelly sandwich!

Winter Squash Bread

Of all the recipes you can make with Acorn or Butternut Squash, this bread has to be the easiest and one of the tastiest, in my opinion. The cozy flavors of fall and winter bake beautifully together in this tender and delicious loaf; serve with apple butter for a scrumptious treat!

Ingredients:

1 ½ c. all-purpose flour
1 c. granulated sugar
1 tsp. baking soda
¼ tsp. baking powder
½ tsp. salt
½ tsp. ground cinnamon
½ tsp. nutmeg
1 c. cooked, mashed butternut or acorn squash
2 eggs, beaten
¼ c. melted butter

Instructions:

1. Preheat oven to 350 degrees.
2. In a large mixing bowl, combine the dry ingredients and whisk until evenly blended.
3. In a separate bowl, combine the mashed squash, eggs and butter.
4. Add the wet ingredients to the dry ingredients; stir just until dry ingredients are moistened evenly.
5. Pour mixture into a greased and floured 8 x 4 x 2-inch loaf pan.
6. Bake for 50 to 60 minutes, or until a toothpick inserted into the center comes out clean.
7. Cool in pan for 10 minutes, and then remove to a wire rack to cool completely. Enjoy!

Yield: 1 loaf

★★★

confections
~~Confessions~~ of a Seasonal Foodie:

★★★

Scrumptious Sweets

and

Tantalizing Treats!

★★★

Sweets and Treats:

Apple and Mincemeat Pie

Mincemeat is one of my favorite ingredients to bake with during the cool seasons. Don't let the name fool you, it is packed with a cozy blend of flavorful fruit and spices! If you like fruity pies, you will love this one!

Ingredients:

Pastry for 2-crust pie
3 medium tart baking apples, peeled, cored, thinly sliced
2/3 c. snipped dried apricots
3 tbsp. all-purpose flour
2 tbsp. unsalted butter, melted, cooled
1 (27 oz.) jar ready-to-use mincemeat
½ c. chopped pecans
1 egg yolk, plus 1 tbsp. water

Instructions:

1. Place rack in lower half of oven. Preheat oven to 425 degrees.
2. In a large mixing bowl, toss apples and apricots with flour and butter.
3. Turn mixture into the prepared pie crust. Spoon mincemeat evenly over apple and apricot mixture. Top with pecans.
4. Place top crust over filling; trim and flute edges. Cut slits in top crust.
5. In a small bowl, beat together the egg yolk and water; brush over crust.
6. Bake at 425 for 10 minutes, then reduce oven temperature to 375 and continue baking for an additional 25 minutes or until golden.
7. Cool to room temperature, cover and chill prior to serving. Enjoy!

Yield: 8 servings

Kitchen Kimberley's Tips:

❖ To substitute condensed mincemeat for ready-to-use mincemeat, crumble 1 (9 oz.) package condensed mincemeat into a small saucepan; add ¾ cup water. Boil briskly for 1 minute. Cool, and proceed as recipe directs.

❖ Store this pie in the refrigerator for best quality.

Apple Brownies

These tender, chewy brownies will melt in your mouth! Their buttery-brown sugar goodness is perfectly balanced by the tartness of the fresh apple. These make a great after-school snack for the kids!

Ingredients:

2/3 c. unsalted butter
1 c. brown sugar
1 c. granulated sugar
2 eggs
1 tsp. vanilla
1 ½ c. all-purpose flour
2 tsp. baking powder
¼ tsp. salt
1 c. peeled, chopped Granny Smith apple
1 c. chopped pecans or walnuts

Instructions:

1. Preheat oven to 350 degrees.
2. In a large mixing bowl, mix butter, sugars, eggs and vanilla. Stir in flour, baking powder and salt.
3. Fold in apples and nuts.
4. Spread mixture into a greased 9 x 9 x 2-inch baking pan.
5. Bake for 35 to 40 minutes, or until a toothpick inserted into the center comes out clean. Enjoy!

Yield: 8 servings

Kitchen Kimberley's Tips:

❖ When baking a recipe that calls for butter, it is best to use unsalted, especially if salt is also listed as an ingredient. Using unsalted butter allows you to better control the amount of salt, and results in the best flavor.

❖ Granny Smith apples are commonly used in baking; their firm texture holds up very well to heat, but there are other great apples for baking, too. Try Cortland, Empire or Jonathan for a change.

Apple Pie with Candied Crust

This old-fashioned favorite has been in my family for many generations.   I cannot even begin to count the times that I have made and enjoyed this recipe! It is simple to make, and simply irresistible when served with freshly whipped cream.

Ingredients:

1 (20 oz.) can apple pie filling
1 c. firmly packed light brown sugar
1 c. all-purpose flour
½ tsp. salt
½ tsp. cinnamon
½ c. butter, softened

Instructions:

1. Preheat oven to 350 degrees.
2. Spread apple pie filling in a 9-inch pie plate.
3. In a medium mixing bowl, combine dry ingredients; cut in butter using a pastry cutter.
4. Spread mixture evenly over apple pie filling.
5. Bake for 45 minutes.
6. Serve warm with softened vanilla ice cream or whipped cream   Enjoy!

Yield: 6 servings

Kitchen Kimberley's Tips:

❖ Try using Cherry or Blueberry Pie filling for a tasty variation, but leave out the cinnamon!

❖ No pastry knife in your kitchen drawer? No problem! Use two butter knives in a criss-cross fashion to cut the butter into your dry ingredients.

Autumn Surprise Cake

You will be surprised at how much people rave when you serve this moist, delicious cake!

Cake Ingredients:

2 c. peeled, cored, chopped baking apples
1 c. granulated sugar
1 ½ c. all-purpose flour
1 tsp. baking soda
1 tsp. vanilla
½ tsp. salt
½ c. vegetable oil
1 egg, beaten
½ c. chopped pecans or walnuts
½ c. flaked coconut

Cake Instructions:

1. Preheat oven to 350 degrees. In a large mixing bowl, combine apples and sugar; let stand until juice forms.
2. Meanwhile, sift dry ingredients, and then add to juicy apple mixture.
3. Add egg, oil, nuts and coconut, blending well.
4. Pour mixture into a greased and floured 9-inch round cake pan.
5. Bake for 40 to 45 minutes; cool before icing.

Vanilla Icing Ingredients:

1 c. brown sugar
3 tbsp. butter
¼ c. milk
½ c. powdered sugar
1 tsp. vanilla
½ c. chopped pecans or walnuts

Vanilla Icing Instructions:

1. In a saucepan over medium heat, mix brown sugar, butter and milk; bring mixture to a boil, and boil for only one minute.
2. Carefully stir in powdered sugar and vanilla; remove from heat.
3. Beat icing until smooth and thick enough to spread onto cake.
4. Spread icing onto cake and then sprinkle with chopped nuts.

Butterscotch Apple Crumb Pie

The mere thought of this pie makes my mouth water!   I cannot say any more!

Ingredients:

1 ½ tsp. lemon juice
4 c. peeled, cored, and sliced tart cooking apples
½ c. granulated sugar
¼ c. all-purpose flour
1 tsp. cinnamon
1/8 tsp. salt
1 (9-inch) unbaked pie shell

Instructions:

1. Preheat oven to 375 degrees.
2. In a large bowl, combine lemon juice and apples; toss until well coated.
3. Stir in sugar, flour, cinnamon, and salt; mix well. Turn into an unbaked pie shell.
4. Cover edges of pie crust with foil to prevent overbrowning, if desired.
5. Bake for 20 minutes. Meanwhile, prepare butterscotch topping.

Butterscotch Topping Ingredients:

6 oz. butterscotch baking morsels
¼ c. butter
¾ c. all-purpose flour
1/8 tsp. salt

Butterscotch Topping Instructions:

1. In a bowl over hot, not boiling water, melt the butterscotch morsels and butter; stir until smooth.
2. Remove from heat; stir in flour and salt. Blend until mixture forms large crumbs.
3. Crumble mixture over top of hot apples, and continue baking for an additional 20 to 25 minutes.

Kitchen Kimberley's Tip:

- ❖ The topping can also be made directly in a small saucepan over low heat; just be sure not to scorch the morsels, and it will work just fine.

Butterscotch Bars

These bars may remind you of a similar 'crispy treat', but the Butterscotch flavor sets them miles apart! These are a great way to get your kids in the kitchen, too; they will have fun pressing the mixture into the pan!

Ingredients:

1 (7 oz.) jar marshmallow crème
2 tbsp. water
2 tbsp. light corn syrup
1 (12 oz.) pkg. butterscotch morsels
8 c. crispy rice cereal
1 c. salted peanuts

Instructions:

1. In a heavy saucepan, combine marshmallow crème, water and corn syrup; heat and stir over medium heat until mixture comes just to a boil.
2. Remove from heat; add butterscotch morsels, stirring until thoroughly blended.
3. In a large mixing bowl, combine crispy rice cereal and peanuts.
4. Pour marshmallow mixture over cereal and nuts; stir until cereal is well coated.
5. Press mixture firmly into a very well buttered 9 x 13 x 2-inch pan.
6. Chill until firm; cut into squares for serving. Enjoy!

Yield: 12 servings or more depending on serving size

Kitchen Kimberley's Tip:

❖   For an easy variation, substitute peanut butter morsels or milk chocolate morsels for the butterscotch morsels. Enjoy your *Peanut Butter Bars* or *Chocolate Bars!*

Cake Mix Snickerdoodles

Snickerdoodles always remind me of my childhood because they were frequently served in our elementary school cafeteria. Now that I am all grown up, I enjoy baking this simplified version of the old-fashioned recipe. It tastes just as good as the original, but only takes a fraction of the time to make!

Ingredients:

1 box yellow cake mix
2 eggs
1 stick butter, melted
Sugar and cinnamon, mixed to taste

Instructions:

1. Preheat oven to 375 degrees.
2. In a large bowl, mix together the dry cake mix, eggs and butter.
3. Shape mixture into 1-inch balls.
4. Roll balls in sugar and cinnamon mixture.
5. Place balls on cookie sheet about 2 inches apart.
6. Flatten gently with a glass dipped in the sugar and cinnamon mixture.
7. Bake for 8 to 10 minutes; cool on baking sheet for 2 minutes.
8. Remove to a wire rack to cool completely. Enjoy!

Kitchen Kimberley's Tip:

❖ The best way to mix this dough is with your (clean!) hands. The warmth of your hands helps to melt the butter and blend the ingredients evenly.

Candied Pecans

These irresistible treats were always available at my Mom's house. If there wasn't a fresh batch made, you could find one in the freezer, and they were all simply scrumptious! When my sister Sabrina visited from Texas, Mom always made an extra batch to send back for my nephew, John. He just loved getting those special sweet treats from his Grandma Jo, and she loved making them for him and for everyone else, too! I hope you enjoy these family treats as much as we do!

Ingredients:

1 egg white
½ tsp. vanilla
¾ c. packed light brown sugar
2 c. pecan halves

Instructions:

1. Generously grease a baking sheet; set aside.
2. Preheat oven to 250 degrees.
3. In a large mixing bowl, beat egg white until it stands in soft peaks; gradually mix in brown sugar and vanilla.
4. Fold in pecans, making sure that all halves are completely covered.
5. Using 2 forks, remove the coated pecans, one at a time, and place one-inch apart on the prepared baking sheet.
6. Bake in preheated oven for 30 minutes, and then turn oven off and leave candy in oven for another 30 minutes; do not open the oven door during this time.
7. Remove candy from oven and allow them to cool to room temperature. Enjoy! Store in an airtight container.

Yield: Approximately 36 pieces

Kitchen Kimberley's Tips:

❖ Candied Pecans freeze very well in an airtight container or freezer bag.

❖ When presented in a pretty tin or a glass jar, this candy makes a great gift from the kitchen!

Caramel Apple Coffee Cake

When this coffee cake is on the brunch table at my house, there is never a crumb left! We love to enjoy this on holiday mornings with sausage or bacon and fresh seasonal fruits. It is best made a day in advance, which makes it perfect for holiday entertaining or weekend guests.

Ingredients:

½ c. shortening
1 c. granulated sugar
2 eggs
1 tsp. vanilla
2 c. all-purpose flour
½ tsp. salt
1 tsp. baking soda
1 c. sour cream
2 c. peeled and chopped baking apples
½ c. chopped pecans
½ c. light brown sugar
1 tsp. ground cinnamon
2 tbsp. melted butter
Garnish: Caramel ice cream topping, whipped cream, and chopped pecans, to taste

Instructions:

1. Preheat oven to 350 degrees.
2. In a large mixing bowl, cream together the shortening and sugar.
3. Add eggs and vanilla; beat well; stir in flour, salt and baking soda.
4. Next, add sour cream and then fold in the apples. Spread mixture into a well-greased 9 x 13 x 2-inch baking pan.
5. For topping, combine the chopped pecans, brown sugar, cinnamon and melted butter; sprinkle evenly over the batter in pan.
6. Bake for 35 to 40 minutes or until a toothpick comes out clean.
7. To serve, cut cake into squares. Place a 'puddle' of caramel topping onto serving plate; set cake atop.
8. Top with a dollop of whipped cream, sprinkle with chopped pecans, and then drizzle with more caramel topping. Oh my goodness! Enjoy!

Yield: 12 servings

Carrot and Zucchini Bars

What a delicious way to eat vegetables! These moist, flavorful bars are great as an after-school snack with a tall glass of cold milk. Both kids and adults alike will gobble them up quickly!

Ingredients:

1 ½ c. all-purpose flour
1 tsp. baking powder
½ tsp. ground ginger
¼ tsp. baking soda
2 eggs, slightly beaten
1 ½ c. grated carrot (about 3 medium)
1 c. grated zucchini (about 1 medium)
¾ c. packed light brown sugar
½ c. raisins
½ c. chopped walnuts
½ c. vegetable oil
¼ c. honey
1 tsp. vanilla
8 oz. cream cheese, softened
1 c. powdered sugar
1 tsp. finely grated lemon or orange zest

Instructions:

1. Preheat oven to 350 degrees.
2. In a large bowl, combine flour, baking powder, ginger, and baking soda.
3. In another large bowl, stir together eggs, carrot, zucchini, brown sugar, raisins, walnuts, oil, honey and vanilla.
4. Add carrot mixture to flour mixture, stirring just until combined. Spread batter into an ungreased 9 x 13 x 2-inch baking pan.
5. Bake 25 minutes, or until a toothpick inserted near the center comes out clean; cool in pan on a wire rack.
6. Meanwhile, to prepare frosting, in a large bowl beat the cream cheese and powdered sugar with an electric mixer on medium speed until fluffy. Stir in the citrus zest. Spread frosting over cooled cake and then cut into bars. Store in an airtight container in the refrigerator. Enjoy!

Kitchen Kimberley's Tip:

❖ For a variation, try using golden raisins and chopped pecans.

Chocolate Chip Cookies

My family has enjoyed these cookies since before I was even born! Over the years, my Mom probably baked a million of these, literally! I cannot remember a time when the cookie jar was not full of these buttery chocolate delights. My Mom sent a bag full of these cookies with Terry and me on our first date to an air show. The cookies sat in the car most of the day, and were warm and gooey when we finally ate them! Terry likes to joke that these cookies are the reason why he asked me out again. Well...you know what they say...the way to a man's heart is through his stomach! I am so thankful that it worked for me!   *Yield: 7 dozen cookies*

Ingredients:

2/3 c. shortening
2/3 c. butter, softened
1 c. granulated sugar
1 c. packed light brown sugar
2 eggs
2 tsp. vanilla
3 c. all-purpose flour
1 tsp. baking soda
1 tsp. salt
1 c. chopped nuts
12 oz. semisweet chocolate chips

Instructions:

1. Preheat oven to 350 degrees.
2. In a large mixing bowl, cream the shortening, butter and sugars together well; add eggs and vanilla, mix thoroughly.
3. In a separate bowl, combine the flour, baking soda, and salt; add dry ingredients to wet mixture, blending well.
4. Stir in nuts and chocolate chips by hand.
5. Drop dough by rounded teaspoonfuls 2-inches apart onto an ungreased baking sheet.
6. Bake for 8 to 10 minutes or until light brown; cool slightly before removing to a wire rack to cool completely. Enjoy!

Kitchen Kimberley's Tip:

❖ Baked cookies can be stored in an airtight container for several weeks, or in the freezer for up to six months.

Coffee Crunch Bars

These delicious cookie bars are reminiscent of a chocolate chip cookie, but the distinguishing coffee flavor makes them very unique! With simple and quick preparation, these are my 'go-to' treat for unexpected visitors. Serve them with a hot cup of coffee or cappuccino for a scrumptious snack.

Ingredients:

1 c. all-purpose flour
½ c. packed light brown sugar
½ c. unsalted butter, softened to room temperature
3 tsp. instant coffee granules
¼ tsp. baking powder
1/8 tsp. salt
½ tsp. vanilla
¼ c. chopped walnuts or pecans
½ c. semisweet chocolate chips

Instructions:

1. Preheat oven to 350 degrees.
2. In a large mixing bowl, combine flour, sugar, butter, coffee granules, baking powder salt and vanilla. Stir in nuts and chocolate chips; batter will be thick.
3. Press mixture evenly into an ungreased 9 x 9 x 2-inch baking pan.
4. Bake until light brown and crisp, about 25 to 30 minutes.
5. Cut into bars, 3 x 1 ½ inches, while bars are still warm.

Yield: 18 bars

Kitchen Kimberley's Tips:

❖ It is not a misprint; there are no eggs in this recipe!

❖ Try a variation with butterscotch chips or toffee bits instead of the chocolate chips.

❖ This recipe can also be made with instant Cappuccino powder in place of the instant coffee granules. Enjoy your *'Cappuccino Crunch Bars'*!

Cranberry Pie

Simple to make, and simply delicious! The tender topping adds the perfect amount of sweetness to these tart little gems. On a chilly fall evening, this is a fabulous dessert to warm you up!

Ingredients:

2 c. whole cranberries
½ c. granulated sugar
½ c. chopped pecans
2 eggs
1 c. all-purpose flour
1 c. granulated sugar
½ c. butter, melted
¼ c. shortening, melted

Instructions:

1. Preheat oven to 325 degrees.
2. Grease a 10" pie plate well.
3. Spread cranberries over the bottom of the pie plate; sprinkle with ½ cup of sugar and chopped nuts.
4. In a mixing bowl, beat the eggs well; add remaining cup of sugar to eggs and mix well.
5. Next, add flour, melted butter and shortening to eggs and sugar mixture; mix well, and then pour over berries in pan.
6. Bake for 1 hour or until lightly browned on top. Enjoy!

Yield: 6 servings

Kitchen Kimberley's Tips:

❖ This pie is best served warm, and is especially good when served with vanilla ice cream.

❖ How can you tell if your cranberries are fresh? See if they bounce! I know, it sounds crazy, but it is true. In fact, they were once referred to as 'bounce berries'!

Crock Pot Caramel Apples

For casual fall entertaining, place caramel coated apples (through step 5) on a table set up with a variety of garnishes. Upon arrival, allow guests to decorate their own apples and put them back into the refrigerator. After dinner, guests can enjoy their very own creation for dessert!

Ingredients:

2 (14 oz.) pkgs. caramels, unwrapped
¼ c. water
8 large apples of your choice
8 Popsicle sticks (usually included with the bags of caramels)

Optional garnishes:

- Melted chocolate – white, milk, dark...all good choices!
- Melted butterscotch or peanut butter morsels
- Chopped nuts – cashews, pecans, macadamia nuts
- Candies, crushed cookies, toasted coconut, etc.

Instructions:

1. Place caramels and water into crock pot; set on high heat for 1 to 1 ½ hours, stirring frequently.
2. Meanwhile, wash and dry apples thoroughly; place popsicle sticks firmly into apples through stem end.
3. Line a baking sheet with parchment paper and set aside.
4. When caramel is melted and smooth, dip apples to coat evenly; holding apples over crock pot, scrape off any excess caramel.
5. Place coated apples onto baking sheet lined with parchment paper; refrigerate for 30 to 60 minutes to set up. Check after 30 minutes to see how caramel is sticking to apples; if it starts to pool at the bottom, simply wet your hands and mold the caramel back where you want it to be. Chill until set.
6. Drizzle or dip into melted chocolate, then garnish as desired by rolling into chopped candies, nuts, etc. Get creative!
7. Store in refrigerator until ready to serve. Enjoy!

Yield: 8 servings

Crunchy Caramel Apple Pie

My sweet cousin Linda shared this recipe with me after she served it years ago at our family reunion. On that day it was the first dessert to be devoured, and after tasting this pie, you will understand why!

Ingredients:

1 refrigerated pie crust
½ c. granulated sugar
3 tbsp. all-purpose flour
1 tsp. ground cinnamon
1/8 tsp. salt
6 c. thinly sliced, peeled cooking apples
1 c. packed light brown sugar
½ c. all-purpose flour
½ c. quick-cooking oats
½ c. butter
½ c. chopped pecans
¼ c. caramel ice cream topping

Instructions:

1. Preheat oven to 375 degrees.
2. Line a 9-inch pie plate with refrigerated pie crust; trim edges and flute, if desired.
3. In a large mixing bowl, stir together sugar, flour, cinnamon and salt; add apple slices and gently toss until coated.
4. Transfer apple mixture to pie crust, spreading evenly.
5. Prepare crumb topping by stirring together the brown sugar, flour and oats. Using a pastry blender, cut in the butter until the mixture resembles coarse crumbs. Sprinkle crumb topping over apple mixture.
6. To prevent overbrowning, cover edge of pie with a foil sleeve. Bake for 25 minutes; remove foil, and continue baking for 25 to 30 minutes more or until the top is golden.
7. Remove from oven, sprinkle pie with chopped pecans, and then drizzle with caramel topping. Cool, and enjoy!

Yield: 8 servings

Divine Divinity

Every Christmas the ladies in my family gather for what we call 'marathon baking and candy making days'! We each select our favorite recipes and together we make them while sipping hot cocoa and listening to holiday music. It is a joyous time filled with fun, laughter, and lots of delicious holiday treats! This melt-in-your-mouth candy, my brother's personal favorite, is always part of the festivities!

Ingredients:

2 2/3 c. granulated sugar
2/3 c. light corn syrup
½ c. water
2 egg whites, at room temperature
1 tsp. vanilla
2/3 c. chopped nuts

Instructions:

1. Line a large baking sheet with waxed paper and set aside. Butter the tip of 2 teaspoons and set aside for dropping prepared candy.
2. In a 2-quart heavy saucepan over medium heat, stir sugar, corn syrup and water until sugar is dissolved. Once sugar is dissolved, carefully attach a candy thermometer to the side of the pan, making sure that the bulb is immersed, but not touching the bottom of the pan.
3. Cook mixture, without stirring, to 260 degrees on candy thermometer, adjusting heat as necessary to maintain a steady boil.
4. Meanwhile, in a mixing bowl beat egg whites until stiff peaks form.
5. Continue beating while slowly and carefully pouring the hot syrup in a thin stream into the egg whites.
6. Add vanilla, beat until mixture holds its shape and becomes slightly dull; fold in nuts.
7. Using the two buttered teaspoons, quickly drop divinity onto waxed paper – lined sheets. Enjoy!

Kitchen Kimberley's Tips:

❖ Candy-making turns out best on non-humid days. However, if you decide to make this recipe on a damp or humid day, simply reduce the amount of water by one tablespoon.

❖ If desired, add food coloring according to your taste when you add the vanilla. Just a few drops can make beautiful candy!

Holiday Corn Flake Wreaths

Every time I make these I feel like a 5-year-old again! My Mom and I used to make these together when she was a Room Mother for my elementary classes. We made these for class holiday parties every year, and I still enjoy them just the same. They are a little messy, but they are so much fun to make and eat!

Ingredients:

½ c. butter
1 (10 oz.) pkg. regular marshmallows
1 tsp. green food coloring
6 c. corn flake cereal
Red cinnamon candies
Vegetable cooking spray

Instructions:

1. In a large saucepan, melt butter over low heat. Add marshmallows and stir until completely melted. Remove from heat; stir in food coloring.
2. Add cereal and stir until evenly coated.
3. Using ¼-cup dry measuring cup coated with cooking spray, evenly portion warm cereal mixture onto a baking sheet lined with parchment paper. Using buttered fingers, quickly shape into individual wreaths. Dot with cinnamon candies for garnish. Enjoy! Store in an airtight container.

Kitchen Kimberley's Tips:

❖ When I was little, there was no such thing as a *microwave*; but now, this recipe is even easier to prepare, thanks to that very common household appliance!

❖ To prepare this treat in the microwave, simply combine the butter and marshmallows in a large microwave-safe bowl; heat on HIGH power for 2 minutes; stir to combine well. Microwave at HIGH power 1 minute longer, then stir in food coloring and continue with steps 2 and 3 as instructed above.

❖ When storing these cookies, separate each layer with a piece of waxed or parchment paper.

Honey Bun Cake

Whether you serve this for brunch or as a holiday dessert, you will certainly receive rave reviews! This is a 'must-have' treat for our holiday brunches!

Ingredients:

1 pkg. yellow cake mix
½ c. granulated sugar
2/3 c. canola oil
4 large eggs
1 c. sour cream (not light or fat-free!)
½ c. packed light brown sugar
2 tsp. ground cinnamon
1 c. powdered sugar
¼ c. milk

Instructions:

1. Preheat oven to 350 degrees.
2. In a large mixing bowl, combine the cake mix, sugar, oil, eggs and sour cream; mix well.
3. In a small bowl, combine the brown sugar and cinnamon; mix well.
4. Pour half of the cake mix batter into a greased 9 x 13 x 2-inch baking pan; sprinkle half of the cinnamon mixture over the batter.
5. Add remaining batter; sprinkle with the remaining cinnamon mixture.
6. Swirl batter back and forth with a knife.
7. Bake for 35 minutes.
8. Combine the powdered sugar and milk; pour over the warm cake. Enjoy!

Yield: 12 servings

Kitchen Kimberley's Tips:

❖ Serving this for brunch? Prepare cake a day in advance, cover and allow the flavors to mingle overnight. It is delicious served warm or at room temperature.

❖ Love cinnamon? Add ½ teaspoon ground cinnamon to the glaze mixture.

Honey Chocolate Sauce

How can three ingredients come together so perfectly? Try it and see! This is my husband's favorite chocolate sauce; sometimes I think he could eat a whole bowl of this all by itself, but he typically enjoys it over cakes or ice cream, even in the winter! Served warm, it is delightfully rich and smooth, and perfect for topping a dessert of almost any type!

Ingredients:

1 (6 oz.) pkg. semi-sweet chocolate chips
½ c. honey
¾ c. evaporated milk

Instructions:

1. In a small saucepan over low heat, melt and stir the chocolate chips and honey until well blended.
2. Stir in the evaporated milk and mix well until smooth. Remove from heat, and allow sauce to cool to room temperature, or serve slightly warm, if desired. Store in refrigerator. Enjoy!

Yield: 1 ¾ cups

Kitchen Kimberley's Tips:

❖ The serving possibilities with this sauce are simply endless! It can dress up any store-bought dessert when you are short on time. Try spooning it over a slice of plain cheesecake. Call it *'Chocolate Drenched Cheesecake'* and enjoy the rave reviews! For fun, top it off with crumbled toffee candy bars for even more decadence!

❖ Another way to enjoy this creamy chocolate sauce is as a fondue. Serve it with cubes of pound cake, fresh strawberries, or pretzel rods for a rich and creamy treat!

Macadamia Nut Pie

Fall and winter are wonderful seasons in which to bake nut pies, and while most people are serving pecan and walnut pies, you can delight everyone with this unusual and scrumptious Macadamia Nut Pie!

Ingredients:

1 refrigerated pie crust
1 c. light corn syrup
3 tbsp. unsalted butter
½ c. light brown sugar
3 tbsp. all-purpose flour
¼ tsp. salt
3 eggs
1 ½ tsp. vanilla extract
1 (6 ½ oz.) jar macadamia nuts, coarsely chopped

Instructions:

1. Preheat oven to 350 degrees.
2. Place the pie crust in a 9-inch pie plate or tart pan, pressing the crust firmly into the pan. Trim the edges and flute, if desired.
3. In a large saucepan, combine the corn syrup, butter, brown sugar, flour and salt over medium heat, stirring until the mixture comes to a rolling boil. Remove from heat and let cool slightly.
4. Add the eggs and vanilla; mix well. Stir in the macadamia nuts and pour into the pie crust.
5. Bake for 35 to 40 minutes, or until firm.
6. Serve warm or allow pie to cool before slicing and serving. Enjoy!

Yield: 8 servings

Kitchen Kimberley's Tips:

❖ Macadamia nuts have a very high fat content and must be stored carefully to avoid rancidity. Vacuum-packed nuts are the best choice for the freshest product.

❖ Refrigerate unopened nuts in an airtight container up to six months or freeze up to a year. Once opened, refrigerate and use macadamia nuts within two months.

Old-Fashioned Gingersnaps

When the first colorful leaf falls from the big oak tree, it is time to start baking these cookies! They are the epitome of fall baking, and at my house, they are always a treat enjoyed fresh and warm from the oven. Two things always make me think of fall -- football, and these homemade gingersnaps!

Ingredients:

1 c. granulated sugar
¾ c. shortening
1 egg
¼ c. molasses
2 c. all-purpose flour
1 tbsp. ground ginger
2 tbsp. baking soda
1 tsp. ground cinnamon
½ tsp. salt
About ½ cup granulated sugar to roll cookies in before baking.

Instructions:

1. Preheat oven to 350 degrees.
2. In a large mixing bowl, cream the sugar and shortening well.
3. Beat in the egg and molasses.
4. Next, add the flour, ginger, baking soda, cinnamon and salt; blend well.
5. Form about a teaspoon of dough into small balls by rolling lightly between palms of hands.
6. Place sugar in a small bowl; roll dough balls gently in sugar to cover entire surface.
7. Place balls 2 inches apart on ungreased cookie sheet.
8. Bake for 12 minutes for a softer cookie, and up to 15 minutes for a crisp texture. Cool on baking sheet for 2 minutes, and then transfer to a wire rack to cool completely. Enjoy!

Yield: 5 dozen cookies

Kitchen Kimberley's Tips:

❖ These can also be made into big 'bakery-style' cookies! Use ¼ cup of dough for each cookie, flatten slightly and bake for about 20 minutes. My family loves these *Giant Gingersnaps*!

Old-Fashioned Peanut Butter Fudge

Holidays would not be the same without fudge, and this old-fashioned peanut butter version is always loved by everyone! Cut this fudge into small squares, as it is very rich!

Ingredients:

1 (7 oz.) jar marshmallow crème
1 c. creamy peanut butter
1 ½ c. granulated sugar
¾ c. evaporated milk
1 tsp. vanilla
½ c. chopped peanuts

Instructions:

1. Grease a 9-inch square pan; set aside.
2. Place marshmallow crème and peanut butter into a large mixing bowl; blend together by hand very well.
3. Add sugar and evaporated milk to a medium saucepan; attach a candy thermometer to the side, making sure that the bulb is immersed, but not touching the bottom of the pan. Cook over medium-high heat until mixture reaches 238 degrees, which is soft ball stage.
4. Remove from heat; stir in vanilla and carefully pour hot mixture over the peanut butter mixture in bowl. Mix well by hand, until creamy. Pour into prepared pan. Sprinkle evenly with chopped peanuts, and allow fudge to cool completely. Enjoy!

Yield: 24 servings

Kitchen Kimberley's Tip:

❖ An accurate candy thermometer is a candy-maker's best friend! Test your candy thermometer by carefully inserting the bulb into a pan of boiling water; it should read 212 degrees. If not, it is time for a new candy thermometer!

Orange Fruit Cake

By far, this is the best fruit cake I have ever tasted! If you like citrus, you will love it!

Cake Ingredients:

1 lb. orange candy slices
1 lb. pitted dates
2 c. coarsely chopped pecans
4 c. all-purpose flour
2 sticks butter, softened to room temperature
2 c. granulated sugar
1 1/3 c. buttermilk, *divided use*
4 eggs
½ tsp. baking soda

Glaze Ingredients:

1 (6 oz.) can orange juice concentrate, thawed
2 c. packed light brown sugar

Instructions:

1. Dice orange slices and dates and place into a large mixing bowl with the chopped pecans. Sift the flour over them, toss to coat and set aside.
2. Preheat oven to 275 degrees. In a large mixing bowl, cream the butter and sugar; add eggs, one at a time, beating well after each addition.
3. Add 1 cup of the buttermilk; stir baking soda into remaining 1/3 cup of buttermilk and then add to batter, mix well. Stir in flour mixture and blend well.
4. Pour batter into a greased and floured 10-inch tube pan, or into 2 greased and floured (9 x 5-inch) loaf pans. Bake for about 2 hours, or until light golden brown on top.
5. Meanwhile, combine glaze ingredients in a bowl and pour half of the mixture over the cake as soon as it comes out of the oven. Let cake stand for 5 to 7 minutes, and then turn out onto a wire rack. Pour remaining glaze over the cake; cool completely.
6. Cover cake tightly in foil and refrigerate until ready to serve. Enjoy!

Kitchen Kimberley's Tip:

❖ This fruitcake can be enjoyed immediately, or sliced throughout the holiday season as a sweet treat.

Peanut Brittle

A staple recipe for anyone who makes candy, this old-fashioned peanut brittle is quite simple to make, and completely irresistible! Every year I plan to give some as holiday gifts, but somehow it disappears before that can happen! I love this recipe!

Ingredients:

½ c. light corn syrup
¼ c. cold water
½ c. granulated sugar
½ c. firmly packed brown sugar
1 c. raw peanuts
2 tbsp. butter, softened
1 tsp. baking soda
1 tsp. vanilla

Instructions:

1. Grease a large cookie sheet, and place in a warm (250 degree) oven.
2. In a 2-quart saucepan over medium-high heat, combine the corn syrup, water and sugars; stir until sugar is dissolved.
3. Attach a candy thermometer to the side of the pan, making sure that the bulb is immersed, but not touching the bottom of the pan.
4. Cook, stirring frequently, until mixture reaches 250 degrees. Add peanuts and continue cooking until temperature reaches 300 degrees.
5. Immediately stir in butter, baking soda and vanilla; the mixture will foam and bubble. Pour at once onto the warm baking sheet; carefully tilt baking sheet back and forth to spread the brittle evenly.
6. Cool completely, and then snap into serving-sized pieces. Enjoy!

Kitchen Kimberley's Tips:

❖ For a variation, try *Chocolate Covered Peanut Brittle*! Simply drizzle melted chocolate of your choice over the hardened candy, and allow chocolate to set until firm. This works great with dark chocolate, semi-sweet or white chocolate.

❖ Store Peanut Brittle in an airtight container for up to 3 weeks.

Peanut Butter Blossoms

When I was a little girl, I loved to spend weekends with my Aunt Jane and Uncle Dave. Back then, I thought it was fun to sleep on the couch, but I especially loved waking up to a full day of fun in the kitchen with my Aunt Jane! I also remember spending part of the day trying to keep Uncle Dave and my cousins from eating too many of our baked goodies! We had such fun making these cookies as well as many treasured family memories. Thanks Aunt Jane and Uncle Dave!

Ingredients:

½ c. unsalted butter, softened to room temperature
¾ c. smooth peanut butter
1/3 c. packed light brown sugar
1/3 c. granulated sugar
1 large egg
1 tsp. vanilla
2 tbsp. milk
1 ½ c. all-purpose flour
1 tsp. baking soda
½ tsp. salt
Coating: 1/3 c. granulated sugar
Garnish: 48 milk chocolate kisses, unwrapped

Instructions:

1. In a large mixing bowl, beat the butter until smooth. Add the peanut butter and the sugars; beat until light and fluffy, about 3 minutes.
2. Add the egg and vanilla; beat to combine; beat in the milk.
3. In a separate bowl, whisk together the flour, baking soda and salt; add to the peanut butter mixture and beat until incorporated.
4. Cover and chill the batter for about 1 hour, or until firm enough to roll into balls. Meanwhile, line three baking sheets with parchment paper.
5. Preheat oven to 375 degrees.
6. Place the granulated sugar into a small bowl. Roll the batter into 1-inch round balls and roll each ball in the sugar. Place on the prepared baking sheet, spacing about 2-inches apart.
7. Bake the cookies for 8 to 10 minutes, or until they are lightly browned. Immediately upon removing them from the oven, place a chocolate kiss in the center of each cookie, pressing down until the cookie just starts to crack. Cool completely on a wire rack. Enjoy! Makes 4 dozen cookies.

Peanut Butter Granola Bars

These delicious and chewy granola bars are packed with kid-friendly favorites! With chocolate, peanut butter, baking chips and oats, these are not your typical "nice-crispy treat"! Big kids love them, too!

Ingredients:

2 c. quick-cooking oats
2 c. crispy rice cereal
½ c. flaked coconut
½ c. Reese's mini baking pieces
¼ c. raisins
¼ c. mini chocolate chips
2/3 c. packed brown sugar
1/3 c. light corn syrup
1/3 c. honey
2/3 c. crunchy peanut butter
1 tbsp. salted butter
1 tsp. vanilla

Instructions:

1. Spray a 9 x 13 x 2-inch baking dish with non-stick cooking spray; set aside.
2. In a large mixing bowl, combine oats, crispy rice cereal, coconut, baking pieces, raisins, and mini chocolate chips; toss to mix well.
3. Next, in a small saucepan, combine brown sugar, corn syrup and honey over medium heat; bring to a boil, stirring constantly, then remove from heat.
4. Quickly stir in the peanut butter, butter, and vanilla; pour over the oat mixture in bowl, and stir very well to coat evenly.
5. Press mixture firmly into prepared pan. Cover and chill for about 30 minutes, or until set. Cut into desired serving-sized bars and enjoy!
6. Store at room temperature in an air-tight container.

Yield: 12 servings or more depending on serving size

Kitchen Kimberley's Tip:

❖ Wrap these individually for a quick and portable snack on-the-run! They are also great as an after-school snack with a tall glass of cold milk.

Pecan Cream Candy

Candy like this is hard to resist! It tastes almost like a cross between a praline and a piece of divinity, if you can imagine how scrumptious that would be! This recipe is enjoyed by my family every year during the holidays, and everybody loves it!

Ingredients:

2 ½ c. granulated sugar
½ c. evaporated milk
½ c. light corn syrup
½ c. butter
1 tsp. vanilla
2 ½ c. chopped pecans

Instructions:

1. Line a baking sheet with parchment paper; set aside.
2. In a saucepan over medium heat, combine sugar, evaporated milk, corn syrup and butter. Bring mixture to a rolling boil; boil 3 minutes.
3. Remove from heat, add nuts and then vanilla. Beat by hand for 3 to 4 minutes or until mixture starts to look dull.
4. Quickly drop by spoonful onto parchment lined baking sheet. Allow to harden, and enjoy! Store this candy in an airtight container.

Yield: 30 pieces

Kitchen Kimberley's Tips:

- ❖ Like most candy, this turns out best when made on a dry, non-humid day.

- ❖ Make these into the size of candy you like; we typically drop about a tablespoonful of the mixture at a time, so they are bite-sized treats.

- ❖ A simple variation can be made by using walnuts instead of pecans.

Pecan Pie

This is an old-fashioned recipe that my Great Aunt Anna used to make using pecans from the tree in her backyard. We remember her fondly every time we enjoy this delicious pie. Once you have tried this family-favorite recipe, this will surely be your 'forever' Pecan Pie recipe. It is the very best!

Ingredients:

3 eggs
1 c. pancake syrup (use your favorite)
½ c. granulated sugar
4 tbsp. butter, melted and cooled
1 tsp. vanilla extract
1 c. chopped pecans
Pecan halves for garnish, if desired
1 deep dish pie crust, unbaked

Instructions:

1. Preheat oven to 400 degrees.
2. Place pie crust in pan on a foil-lined baking sheet.
3. In a large mixing bowl, beat eggs slightly. Add pancake syrup, granulated sugar, butter and vanilla; blend well.
4. Stir in the chopped pecans, and pour mixture into pie crust.
5. If desired, arrange additional pecan halves in a decorative fashion over the filling.
6. Place a foil sleeve over edges of pie to prevent over-browning during baking.
7. Bake for 10 minutes at 400 degrees, and then lower oven temperature to 325 degrees and bake for an additional 20 minutes with foil sleeve in place.
8. Next, carefully remove the foil sleeve (tongs work well here) and continue baking for another 20 minutes, or until pie is set.
9. Allow pie to cool completely at room temperature, and then store in refrigerator. Enjoy!

Kitchen Kimberley's Tip:

❖ To give your pie a gorgeous glazed look, brush it lightly with warm pancake syrup after it comes out of the oven. This adds a beautiful sheen and scrumptious flavor!

Pumpkin Crisp

Oh...my...goodness! For me, this decadent dessert was love at first bite! One year for Thanksgiving I made a Pecan Pie, a Chocolate Pie, and this Pumpkin Crisp instead of Pumpkin Pie, and this dessert was the first to disappear! Fair warning...it is rich, and quite possibly addictive!

Ingredients:

1 (15 oz.) can pumpkin
1 (12 oz.) can evaporated milk
1 c. granulated sugar
1 tsp. vanilla
½ tsp. cinnamon
1 box butter flavored yellow cake mix
1 c. chopped pecans
1 cup (2 sticks) butter, melted

Instructions:

1. Preheat oven to 350 degrees.
2. Stir together first 5 ingredients; pour mixture into a lightly greased 9 x 13-inch baking dish.
3. Sprinkle cake mix evenly over pumpkin mixture and then sprinkle pecans evenly over cake mix.
4. Drizzle with melted butter.
5. Bake at 350 degrees for 1 hour and 5 minutes (check after 1 hour), or until golden brown.
6. Let stand 10 minutes; serve warm with freshly whipped cream or whipped topping.

Yield: 12 servings

Kitchen Kimberley's Tip:

❖ Baking with real butter is the only way to go, so when it comes to margarine...just say 'no'!

Scrumptious Carrot Cookies

My mouth starts watering at the mere thought of these tender, citrus glazed cookies! When I was growing up my Mom made these all the time, but we especially enjoyed them during the holidays when the oranges were at their peak of flavor. Tins full of these delicious cookies were always well-received holiday gifts from her kitchen!

Cookie Ingredients:

1 c. shortening
¾ c. granulated sugar
1 egg
1 c. cooked and mashed carrots, cooled
2 c. all-purpose flour
2 tsp. baking powder
1 tsp. vanilla
½ tsp. lemon flavoring
1 c. finely chopped pecans

Cookie Instructions:

1. Preheat oven to 350 degrees.
2. In a large mixing bowl, combine the shortening, sugar, egg and cooled carrots; blend very well.
3. Add remaining cookie ingredients and mix thoroughly.
4. Drop cookie dough by heaping teaspoonfuls onto ungreased cookie sheet.
5. Bake 10 to 12 minutes; remove to a wire rack to cool completely.

Icing Ingredients:

Grated rind from one fresh orange
Juice from one fresh orange
1 tbsp. butter, melted
1 box powdered sugar

Icing Instructions:

1. Combine icing ingredients in a mixing bowl, adding the powdered sugar until desired consistency; spread onto cooled cookies. Enjoy!

Sweet Potato Pie

The first time I served this pie to my family it was met with a bit of apprehension simply because of the name. However, after the first bite, Sweet Potato Pie became a name they wanted to remember well, and a taste they will not soon forget! It quickly became a family favorite, and it is now requested frequently!

Ingredients:

3 tbsp. all-purpose flour
1 2/3 c. granulated sugar
1 c. mashed, cooked sweet potatoes
2 eggs
¼ c. light corn syrup
¼ tsp. ground nutmeg
¼ tsp. ground cinnamon
Pinch salt
½ c. unsalted butter
¾ c. evaporated milk
1 unbaked deep dish pastry shell

Instructions:

1. Preheat oven to 350 degrees.
2. In a large mixing bowl, combine the flour and sugar.
3. Add sweet potatoes, eggs, corn syrup, nutmeg, cinnamon, salt, butter and evaporated milk; beat well.
4. Place pastry shell onto a foil-lined baking sheet; pour pie mixture into pastry shell.
5. Bake for 55 to 60 minutes. Cool completely, and refrigerate. Enjoy!

Yield: 8 servings

Kitchen Kimberley's Tip:

❖ Serve this pie with a generous dollop of sweetened whipped cream.

Toffee & Pecan Shortbread Cookies

Shortbread is one of my foodie-addictions! Although I hate to admit it, I have no willpower when presented with the buttery goodness of a shortbread cookie, especially when it is studded with pecans or toffee pieces. One day I decided that the two favorites of mine should come together as one, and oh my – the results were delicious! Toffee and pecans belong together, forever!

Ingredients:

1 c. butter, softened to room temperature
1 tsp. vanilla
½ c. packed light brown sugar
¼ c. packed dark brown sugar
2 ½ c. all-purpose flour
½ c. toffee bits
½ c. chopped pecans

Instructions:

1. In a large mixing bowl, cream together the butter, vanilla and both brown sugars.
2. Add flour, and beat just until mixture is combined; stir in toffee bits.
3. Shape dough into log 1 ½-inches in diameter; wrap in waxed paper and chill for 20 minutes.
4. Meanwhile, preheat oven to 325 degrees and grease 2 large baking sheets.
5. Remove log from waxed paper, and slice into ½-inch thick cookies.
6. Place pecans in a small bowl, and roll the outside edge of each cookie in pecans, coating well; place cookies on greased baking sheets.
7. Bake for 18 to 20 minutes, or until lightly browned.
8. Remove to wire racks to cool completely. Enjoy!

Yield: 24 cookies

Kitchen Kimberley's Tip:

❖ Store cookies in an airtight container with a tight-fitting lid. If they soften, place them in an oven at 300 degrees for 3 to 5 minutes, before serving.

Kitchen Kimberley's Holiday Entertaining Tips:

Presentation:

Everyone will enjoy food that is presented beautifully! When setting up your table to serve 'buffet style', vary the heights of foods by using simple things found around the house, such as phone books, small boxes or even inverted bowls or heavy saucepans. For safety, make sure that the serving dish sits securely atop!

If you do not have coordinating serving dishes, you can easily tie everything together by using a piece of fabric in a complementary color as a table runner. Use a solid color tablecloth as your base cloth, and then gather up the coordinating fabric and lay it down the center of the table to tie the look together.

No-Fuss Appetizers:

❖ Gourmet Cheeses, Dried Fruits, Plain or Sugared Walnuts – when presented on a pretty platter these are irresistible! Add a small bunch of fresh grapes in place of the dried fruits for a variation.

❖ Serve a block of softened cream cheese topped with warmed fruit preserves or jalapeno jelly. Add an assortment of crisp crackers or gingerbread cookies for a delightful sweet treat!

Keep these on hand for last minute get-togethers!

- Frozen pound cake or cheesecake – dress it up with chocolate sauce or caramel sauce
- Frozen blueberries and raspberries; these are great for making a quick sauce to spoon over cakes. Simply heat them in a saucepan with a little maple syrup until warm.
- Specialty crackers or cookies
- Assorted herb flavored cheeses or gourmet cheeses
- Flavored hot teas, coffees, and hot cocoa

Quick Hostess Gifts:

> Glass jar decorated with holiday ribbon and filled with an assortment of nuts.
> Basket filled with specialty teas or coffees and gourmet cookies or chocolates.
> Basket with fresh bagels from the bakery, fancy fruit preserves and fresh fruit.
> Cookbooks (hint hint!!) and unique kitchen gadgets.

Kitchen Kimberley's Top 10 Grocery Savings Tips:

1. Never shop for food when you are hungry!
2. Shop for two weeks of groceries at a time when possible; this habit really lessens impulse shopping.
3. Plan a weekly menu and formulate a shopping list from the meals you will prepare. Shop only from your list!
4. Clip coupons only on the items you typically purchase; use them whenever possible, especially at stores that offer double coupon deals.
5. Purchase 'loss leaders' – these are the items featured on the front and back pages of the grocery circular.
6. Try to purchase more store brands or generic brands. These are often 'co-packed' by the national brand companies and contain the same product, at a much lower price.
7. Compare the 'price per ounce' on the shelf-edge label. The 'economy size' is not always the best deal. Shop with a calculator to find the true bargains.
8. Never buy toiletries at a grocery store or drug store. Get the best deals on these items at the large discount stores; bath soap, shampoo, toothpaste, shaving cream and such can be 20% to 50% less at the big box stores.
9. Check out coupon websites for great deals on common household and food items.
10. Make 'Free Soup' at home! Simply place all leftover cooked vegetables, broth, tomato paste or sauce into a freezer container labeled 'Free Soup'. Freeze, and continue adding leftovers to the container whenever possible. Once the container is full of leftovers, all you have to do is thaw, heat and season according to your taste. Enjoy 'Free Soup'!

Index of *Fabulous Foodie Favorites!*